WARGAME
TERRAIN & BUILDINGS

THE
NAPOLEONIC
WARS

WARGAMES
TERRAIN & BUILDINGS

THE
NAPOLEONIC
WARS

TONY HARWOOD

Pen & Sword
MILITARY

First published in Great Britain in 2019 by
Pen & Sword Military
An imprint of
Pen & Sword Books Ltd
Yorkshire – Philadelphia

ISBN 978 1 52671 639 2

A CIP catalogue record for this book is available from the British Library.

Editing, design and typesetting by Henry Hyde. Typeset in Adobe Caslon Pro,
Gill Sans and Carbon Type
Photography by Tony Harwood unless otherwise credited
Printed and bound in India by Replika Press Pvt. Ltd

Pen & Sword Books Limited incorporates the imprints of Atlas, Archaeology,
Aviation, Discovery, Family History, Fiction, History, Maritime, Military,
Military Classics, Politics, Select, Transport, True Crime, Air World, Frontline
Publishing, Leo Cooper, Remember When, Seaforth Publishing, The Praetorian
Press, Wharncliffe Local History, Wharncliffe Transport, Wharncliffe True
Crime and White Owl.

For a complete list of Pen & Sword titles please contact

PEN & SWORD BOOKS LIMITED
47 Church Street, Barnsley, South Yorkshire, S70 2AS, England
E-mail: enquiries@pen-and-sword.co.uk
Website: www.pen-and-sword.co.uk

Or
PEN AND SWORD BOOKS
1950 Lawrence Rd, Havertown, PA 19083, USA
E-mail: Uspen-and-sword@casematepublishers.com
Website: www.penandswordbooks.com

CONTENTS

INTRODUCTION

I have been building models since I was a teenager, starting with pocket-money Airfix construction kits bought from my local Woolworths, building them in minutes then destroying them in mock battles with my airgun or fireworks. As time went on, I was introduced to both *Dungeons & Dragons* and painting 54mm historical miniatures, producing a hobby that has became a life-long obsession. I believe that this was, in part, due to a father and grandfather who were model makers. Dad built flying scale balsa wood aircraft and also enjoyed the very intricate hobby of putting ships in bottles, and my grandfather had a huge model railway layout in his back bedroom—a layout that I was allowed to both operate and work on.

Much later, as the years passed and I found myself with a growing family, I once again dabbled with both building plastic kits and constructing my own model railway layouts, but I found that it was the scratch-building of individual models and, in particular, the terrain or buildings, that gave me the greatest satisfaction. Fast forward and early retirement meant that I was able to spend much more time on my modelling hobby, producing models for myself as well as masters for commercial companies which have then been moulded and cast in resin.

I have been lucky enough to be published in traditional paper or print magazines as well as internet-only magazines, and the comments that I received on my blog led to me self-publishing a number of model-making guides, as well as becoming a regular contributor to the wargames press.

I have always tried to produce models that have both detail and character; in fact I believe that character is the most important criterion, as a model that has character has so much more to offer to both its creator and the viewer. Because of this, I have always tried to push myself when producing models for books or magazine articles and I believe that it was this drive and attention to detail that led to this (and hopefully further) publication— various themed books on building wargame terrain. It is my hope that I will be able to show some of the many techniques that I use to produce my own wargame terrain, and maybe inspire others to try to produce their own models.

In the past, I would have described myself as a gamer/figure painter. Today, this has changed to being a terrain builder first, a figure painter second and a gamer third. I don't regret this: in fact, I believe that making scratch-built terrain and structures is now my main (and time consuming) hobby. Whether you are looking to start building your own wargame terrain as an add-on to your gaming hobby, just looking for a good read or, like me, you end up building and building and building terrain until your attic has no more room to spare, I hope that you enjoy seeing how I create my wargame terrain.

In this book I will try to include detailed, step-by-step images and text, so that anyone trying to copy the examples shown can build their own models. If you want to tailor the techniques to your own particular style—great. In fact, as you will read, I encourage this.

The techniques used are not new; I have picked them up from others, either by reading about them or asking questions. In fact, I would like to say now that I have had many a fine hour (even hours) chatting away with like-minded individuals who have been only too willing to pass on their knowledge about how to build models, or what materials or tricks they use. In this book, it is my intention to include these hints and tips and pass them on to others who might like to build their own scenery or terrain. Similarly, the materials I use will also be included, and in many cases I will also pass on my money-saving tips of how I can usually build my terrain for mere pennies, using scrap material or ex-advertising material given to me free of charge.

My goal is to build models in a wide range of different scales and materials for various theatres of the Napoleonic Wars. These buildings, although themed to the Napoleonic era, should be of use to gamers and modellers who are looking to produce terrain for other time periods or genres. I am confident that the techniques will allow readers to scratch-build or modify existing kits to any time period or style they want.

It is my intention to include in each tutorial certain key steps: the inspiration for the particular model; the construction; the detailing; the painting and any specific notes or subject matter that I found particularly difficult or unusual.

Finally, I consider myself an average figure painter, but a good terrain painter; it is something about the scale and presence that makes it so much easier for me to paint terrain. I have dabbled with many different painting techniques or styles and, in truth, I am still experimenting—sometimes these experiments don't quite work out as planned, but I treat every mishap as a learning experience. The book will detail the painting steps in just as much detail as the construction steps in the hope that, once again, I can pass on as many hints as possible.

I hope you enjoy it.

Tony Harwood, January 2019

NOTES ON PAINTS USED

I tend to use whatever paint I have to hand: artists' tube acrylic, craft paints, students' acrylic, Games Workshop's Citadel paints (old and new pots), Vallejo and so on—even household emulsion! Throughout this book, I will try to detail the exact paint brand and name, but where this is not possible, I will always revert back to either Vallejo Game Color or Vallejo Model Color. Hopefully, the images will be a guide.

This is not an attempt by me to hide my 'magic paint mixing formulas', it is simply that I don't use paints straight from the bottle or pot. Instead, I mix my own colours, adding a little yellow here or red there to get exactly the colour I want.

I prefer acrylics to oil- or spirit-based paints for two reasons: 1) they dry faster; and 2) they don't smell. Well, most of them don't! I also use a flow improver from Daler Rowney, although you could always add a tiny drop of washing up liquid to your clean water pot. I also have a confession to make; I don't change my water nearly often enough, so even these mixes can be polluted with dirty water!

I do use washes. Some are branded as washes, such as Citadel Washes, whilst others are home-made using Future® floor polish and distilled water as a base. I regularly water down these washes and have no issues with mixing different washes, colours or brands.

My preferred palette is the *Wine and Spirit Guide* published by Waitrose—yes, the supermarket! The pages have a premium gloss finish which acts like a mini 'wet palette'. When I have finished for that session (or colour) I simply tear off the page and I have a new palette. Best of all, they are free!

15mm
RUSSIAN
WINDMILL

1.1
15MM RUSSIAN WINDMILL

WORKING WITH STRIP WOOD

Inspiration

For many years, I had planned to scratch build a traditional wooden or Russian windmill, but had never got around to starting it. This model was inspired by some colour images in a book called *Architecture of the Russian North*, a Russian language book published by Aurora Art Publishing (Leningrad, 1976), full of photographs of now long-forgotten wooden structures, plus some Google image searches on the internet. One of the main reasons for putting off such an undertaking is the sheer size of the model—in 28mm, it would tower over the rest of my gaming table.

While planning this book, I wanted to show a wide range of models built to different scales—a Russian windmill in 15mm would be much more manageable, but even so, this model would still be 200mm tall.

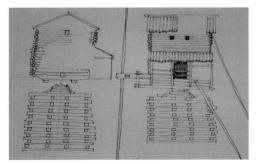

Construction

After producing a simple sketch as a guide, I started with some corrugated cardboard. The individual pieces were cut out and glued together with my hot glue gun.

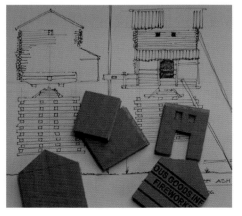

I added strips of torn newspaper which were glued in place with PVA glue.

The base had a second layer of corrugated cardboard added to the lower edges and a balsa wood plug to the top.

I then cut strips of scrap wood into 4mm x 4mm lengths. The wood was picked up free of charge from a local food market—it was once used to transport tangerines. I find that this low quality wood produces superb textures when cut, split and sanded.

These strips were superglued around the cardboard core to produce the alternating, stacked bases of these wooden giants. You should also see how I have used green foam to add shorter sections to the stack. Notice how I have not tried to clean up the exposed edges. This effect will 'pop' when painted and particularly when drybrushed.

The staggered layers continued up the base or tower until I got to about 60mm tall. At this stage, I started to add the wooden strips across the top of the tower and then added a second layer across the first. Once again, construction was done with superglue.

A similar technique could be used to build a Roman brazier or an American Civil War watchtower/signal tower.

I have used DAS modelling clay to fill the gaps between the wooden strips. Remember to apply DAS over a layer of PVA glue. Then a section of (red) knitting needle was first glued and then sandwiched with more wooden strips and DAS.

I have purposely added the DAS in a rough manner, as this is how I would have expected it to have been applied on the original windmill base.

The upper mill was clad with strips of coloured lollipop sticks—for some reason, coloured lollipop sticks are cheaper than plain wood lollipop sticks, so I pick up craft packs or bulk packs of the coloured ones. After all, once painted, no one will know. The lollipop sticks have been given additional texture by scraping with the teeth of a razor saw and then cut freehand, rather than using a straight edge, which would have made them look too uniform.

When the base and the mill are brought together, you can begin to see the effect I was looking for.

The mill was further detailed with more lollipop sticks and Milliput epoxy putty. I have used green foam to model the doorway and split lollipop sticks for the walkway; the wooden strips for the supports under the mill were left over from building the tower base.

The roofs on typical Russian buildings— at least, the ones made of wood—have a shallow, sloping angle and are constructed of wooden boards. I used more of the lollipop sticks yet again to depict this, whilst allowing for the smaller scale.

An additional strip of wood was run along the ridge of the roof and extra strips were added to run from the ridge, down the roof. This feature is seen on many Russian buildings.

I filled any gaps with DAS, then built the lean-to from strip wood and lollipop sticks. I constructed the base from 3mm thick plastic card and built up the groundwork with DAS. I added a trimmed cocktail stick to the top of the base and drilled a hole in the bottom of the mill to act as a pin or swivel. I am still not sure if I will glue these two pieces together or leave them free to revolve.

Detailing

The base was textured with sieved stones, coarse sand and then fine sand. The items of clutter came from my spares box—I chose them with great care to make sure that they were in keeping with the smaller 15mm size. The mill now has a sail spar added although, at this stage, it is not glued in place but

just supported on a cocktail stick axle. The mill and base stand 160mm tall.

I have added tiny nails to the model. These were cut from slivers of plastic card and applied over drops of superglue with the point of a scalpel. I try to add similar surface detail to most of my terrain as I believe it adds interest to the model when painted. I do not try to add every single nail or rivet but

just the impression—I think of it as a "Dampfpanzerwagon" trait and like adding clutter to my bases. It can be seen on many of my scratch-built or customised models. Additional detailing was constructed from more scrap wood.

The Sails

The windmill's wooden sails were constructed from balsa wood. I had thought about making them from plastic card, but the balsa wood was so much easier to work with (although very fragile). I sketched out a simple plan and made all four sails at the same time.

The balsa wood was textured by sanding with some coarse sandpaper and carving with a scalpel. I used superglue to construct the sails and glued them in place on the main axle with a thin piece of wire to pin the sail arms in place.

Once I was happy with the sails, I undercoated the model with a black/dark brown mix, which was applied with a medium-sized brush. I damaged one of the spars during

undercoating and had to make a cocktail stick splint to repair the damage. At this stage, the model is still in three pieces, the base, the mill and the sails.

Painting

The black/brown undercoat was built up with three main colours: Black, Chocolate Brown and Leather Brown. The colours were applied in a haphazard manner and mixed both on the palette and on the model. I used a stiff brush in a 'scrubbing' motion to apply the paint as I needed to get the colour in between the wooden strips.

The first highlight used the same three colours with some Elfic Flesh added to lighten the base colour. I then applied a second highlight, this time using an old standby of mine, Stonewall Grey, to add some aged wood effects. This was drybrushed lightly over the raised detail to pick up on the sculpted texture.

I then washed the model with various washes, some bought like the GW Blue and Black washes and some made using distilled water, a tiny drop of PVA glue and black or brown acrylic paint. When painting aged wood, try not to be restricted to the usual suspects. I regularly apply washes with green, brown and black paint, but purple, red and blue can give some stunning effects too.

Next, one more drybrush, a light drybrush this time. I used more Stonewall Grey, but added some buff/beige to warm the grey and make it less stark.

The groundwork was painted in Leather Brown with some Charred Brown as a shadow. This was lightened with more Leather and Dead White for highlights. The exposed stones in the groundwork were painted with black and white, highlighted with more white added to the mix.

The same groundwork colour was added to parts of the lower tower, where the earth had tumbled out from between the wooden supports.

I then went back over the structures with diluted Leather Brown and Charred Brown to create some variation in the colour of the exposed wood. I try to add a variety of different colours and tones when painting aged wood, making it a 'patchwork' of colours. New wood tends to be cream, older wood more grey and very old wood has a silver tint. This is the effect I was looking to reproduce on this model.

One more light drybrush and the wooden sections are looking finished.

I varnished the whole model and base with Galleria Matt Varnish and then added some dyed sawdust to the base.

The model is not an exact copy of any one windmill, more an amalgamation of many.

The model is built to the (unusual for me) scale of 1/100 to suit 15mm wargame figures. It stands 190mm tall (to the top of the sails) and is mounted on a 3mm thick plastic card base 100mm x 90mm.

Materials used
- Corrugated cardboard
- Card
- Paper
- Balsa wood
- Scrap wood—ex-packing case
- Green foam
- DAS modelling clay
- Milliput (standard green-grey)
- Cocktail stick/skewer
- Knitting needle
- Plastic card
- Plastic rod

- Resin castings
- Sticky-back paper
- Lollipop sticks

Paints used
- Black
- Bestial Brown
- Charred Brown
- Chocolate Brown
- Leather Brown
- Snakebite Leather
- Dead White
- Elfic Flesh
- Stonewall Grey
- Beige
- Hot Orange
- Galleria matt varnish

28/30mm
TWO-STOREY
FRENCH
HOUSE

1.2

28/30MM TWO STOREY FRENCH HOUSE

WHY I ENJOY MAKING BUILDINGS WITH DAS MODELLING CLAY

Inspiration

The inspiration for this structure was found in the Almark Modelling Book No. 9 *Building Napoleonic Dioramas* by Steve Kemp from 1978 (ISBN 0 85524 306 6) and a book on regional French architecture called *The French Farmhouse* by Elsie Burch Donald published in 1995 (ISBN 0 31691226 3).

I picked up this 32-page booklet from a local second-hand book dealer in Tewkesbury for just £1. The techniques, although intended for the novice or beginner, offer some great little starter projects, particularly the two storey French house featured on pages 5-9. I decided that my next project for this book would be a small house based on this design, a simple two storey house with an extension to the right and a set of steps to the left. The

model was never intended to be a straight copy, but does stick to the original design quite closely.

I redrew the design to 1/56th scale to fit in with 28mm or 30mm Napoleonic figures, but found that there was very little difference in size from the drawing featured in the book and my sketch. When planning terrain models it is always a good idea to have a spare miniature to hand, to help with scaling.

Construction

The basic construction was done with some scrap corrugated cardboard which was transferred from the plan and cut out with a large 'snap-off' bladed knife or box cutter. These simple walls were glued together with a hot glue gun to form the cottage shape with the small extension to the side.

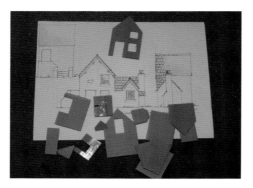

This cardboard core was used to check that the size was correct by placing a 28mm miniature alongside. I have to admit that there have been a few tweaks but the basic shape mirrors both the initial plan and the images in the Almark book.

This cardboard 'blank' was then strengthened with strips of torn-up newspaper applied in layers with PVA glue.

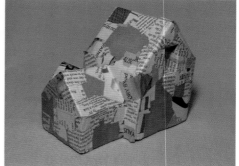

This particular technique of a cardboard core reinforced with paper strips gives a very strong basis for adding subsequent layers of detail but remains light and easy to modify. When placed alongside the initial plans there is very little difference in layout. I did move the main door to the right as I thought is interfered with the stairs and door on the left hand side.

The next image may look the same, but there have been a number of subtle changes. The width has been increased (adding another layer of corrugated cardboard to the left) the upper left window has been filled-in so that a second more centrally placed window opening could be cut into the cardboard at a later date. The small dormer window roof in the extension was first cut off and then placed further to the right to closer resemble the original design while the joins and exposed edges were further re-enforced with strips of newspaper. All of these changes were easy to carry out at this early stage as the core is just corrugated cardboard.

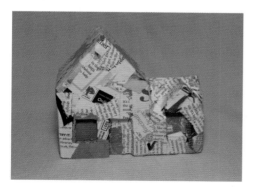

A second door to the left of the building was also added at this stage and the rear of the building has an upper storey access or loft door added, well at least the opening for this door was added. The wooden door will come later.

I then started to clad the external walls with a mix of DAS Terracotta Clay and DAS White Clay. I find that the terracotta variety is slightly smoother and easier to work with, while the white variety does not stain clothes. By mixing my supplies I was able to use up the remainder of an old pack of terracotta clay.

As you can see this first layer is applied quite roughly, I find it better to add DAS Modelling Clay over a thin layer of PVA glue as this helps the DAS to stick and cuts down on the amount of shrinkage.

The model has been refined by adding a chimney to the right hand extension this was constructed from off-cuts of balsa wood which were again covered in DAS. I have marked where I want the new windows to go with a black marker pen.

I started work on the steps to the side, once again balsa wood glued in place with superglue.

Construction continues with the new window opening being cut into the DAS and the cardboard with a scalpel then modelled with more DAS. I have reinforced the interior with additional pieces of corrugated cardboard glued in place with my hot glue gun. The steps to the side have been built-up with more balsa wood and DAS.

In these early images, you can see the different mixes of the terracotta and white DAS that were used. I like to use a 'spear head' shaped metal dentist's tool for most of my sculpting, cutting a small piece of DAS from the packet and then smoothing it on to the model and spreading it out over PVA glue. Once I am happy with the application, I use a large brush soaked in watered-down PVA glue to smooth out the surface.

At this stage of construction I thought I had better place the model onto a base. I prefer to mount my scratch-built terrain onto bases as I think that this helps to make the model sturdier and allows me to add clutter to the base (more on this later). I have used a piece of 3mm plastic card which was originally used as an advertising display board in a DIY store. I draw around the model, making sure to leave enough room for any planned additions to the base and then cut out the rough oval with a large knife. The edges are then chamfered with a knife and later sanded smooth. In this case I glued the building core to the base with a 3mm spacer between the building and the base with superglue. This is an old trick used by diorama modellers to help 'bed' the model (or figure) into the groundwork.

When you look down on the model, you can see just how much room I allowed for the steps and the clutter.

The building and base are then 'bedded-in' with more DAS, once again applied over PVA glue. I like to scratch or score the base with the tip of a scalpel or knife to give the DAS and glue something to 'key' too.

At a late stage, I thought it would add some interest to the steps area by including a cut-out or cellar entrance under the main landing area. Another example of how a model such as this can take on a life of its own as the construction grows. I often change my designs during construction when building scratch-built terrain.

The rear has now had a great deal of DAS added. I thought a partially derelict wall would add to the plain flat rear. Notice how I have allowed the opening for the side door and the rear loft access to extend deep into the model. This is so that the doors appear to be set into the model walls, rather than just lying flat to them. I would suggest that it is easier to over exaggerate these openings and fill them in at a later date, than have a door opening too flush or not deep enough with the exterior walls.

One of the features of the original design was a set of stairs to the side, rising up to an elevated door on the side of the building. These steps have been constructed from sheets of balsa wood and clad in DAS.

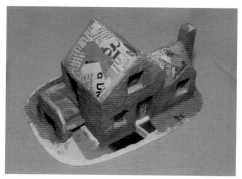

The 'bedding-in' continues with more DAS Modelling Clay and I have added a large step to the main front door.

One quiet evening, I set to finishing off all of the step area and built up the basic shape with balsa wood sheets covered in DAS. It really was a 'suck-it-and-see' exercise but in the end I think I have captured the effect I was looking for. The steps were sculpted in DAS and then placed in the electric oven (on

a low heat) for 10 minutes before DAS was cut away and/or more added. This continued for some time and then when I was happy with the result, I sanded the dried DAS to shape with a home-made sanding stick (3Ms abrasive paper stuck to a strip of scrap of wood with double sided Sellotape).

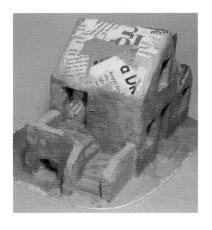

Detailing

With the stairs modelled. I started work on adding some features to the front of the house. The larger corner stones were once again modelled with DAS, the wooden eaves from balsa wood and the small set of white sacks taken from my spares box. Once again, the different mixes of DAS terracotta and DAS white show the layers of clay used on this model. I find it easier to keep adding thin layers than to model a finished design in one go.

The door to the rear loft access was modelled from a single sheet of over-sized balsa wood. I first cut the vertical grooves with a scalpel, then scraped the surface with the teeth of a razor saw and finally brushed the surface in the direct of the grain with some rough sandpaper and/or a wire brush. The door is then cut to size and glued in place before the top, bottom and sides are added from DAS. The ledge to the bottom of the door is added later and again from DAS.

When working on older buildings I have learnt that it is much better NOT to use a straight edge to cut or add detail to the wooden areas—try to impart a slight curve or wobble to any aged timbers as this helps to make the model look more natural. The vertical strips in the loft door and the balsa wood eaves have slight curves purposely included. The next time you are cutting aged timbers, throw away your straight edge and allow the scalpel to wander.

The windows were constructed from Green Foam—foam that is slightly stiffer than the more traditional Blue Foam. I first drew the window design onto some art board (premium card) then added strips of textured green foam glued with superglue. Once the window design was complete, I cut the windows from the art board and glued them into the openings with superglue. Once again, try to vary the style and shape of windows in a design as this also helps to add an impression of run-down buildings to your models, making them appear more natural. The window openings were then defined with DAS.

The main door was constructed from textured green foam, over art board and glued in place with superglue. The wooden beam across the top of the door was modelled from a very thin piece of textured green foam. Note how I have added some nail holes to the wooden window frames. I use a large sewing needle or the point of a dart. (The dart is one of the few tools that I still have from my father's old tool kit—he used it when building ships in bottles.)

The side and elevated door was constructed from balsa wood in the same way as the rear loft door. Once again the doors are of different heights and widths – adding to the individuality of this character piece.

Notice how the balsa wood eaves have had a second layer of balsa wood added to thicken the side profiles. This gives an illusion of thicker or chunkier wood—I glue oversized pieces of balsa wood to the rear of the eaves and when the glue is fully dry, I cut and sand them to shape.

The main door was detailed with a florists' wire door handle (I had seen this feature in a book on Napoleonic uniforms and thought that it would work on this main door). Twist a loop of florists' wire around a drill bit or a needle file and then trim to a loop with a set of nippers. Make a second 'U' shape from the wire and insert this 'U' over the loop and into a pre-drilled hole in the door. Additional detailing as done with plastic rod. Cut the rod into thin slivers and apply superglue to the door with the tip of a wooden cocktail stick. Pick up the plastic rod sliver with the point of a scalpel and apply to the superglue—I find it is a good idea to flood the area with PVA glue when the superglue has fully set.

Longitudinal balsa wood supports have been added to the eaves. This is a feature seen on many early buildings and one that is well worth adding. Different buildings will use square or rectangular sections of timber, some with decorative carvings, so study books on regional architecture to get a 'feel' for the local building style.

Additional rivets or nail heads have been added to the eaves and the door to the side. Try varying their size and shape on different buildings—for example, square-headed nails or small plastic card washers with nails on top.

I have already written of my love of adding 'clutter' to my scratch-built terrain. I have glued some cut logs modelled from balsa wood to the rear of the small extension. These are shaped off-cuts of balsa wood glued in place with superglue and then flooded with dilute PVA glue to ensure that they stay in place. This is an easy modelling project and a feature that could be found on many historical buildings that use wood as fuel. If you have the opportunity to visit a museum such as St Fagans in Wales or Avoncroft Museum in the Midlands, you will find stacks of chopped wood piled up as either stand-alone stacks or against the exhibit buildings.

It's no good, I can't help it... I have carved some exposed stonework to the rear of the extension. I first cut horizontal groves into the DAS, then the vertical grooves with a scalpel. These grooves can be opened out with a large needle or a purpose-made sculpting tool, before being textured by brushing with a wire brush. You can achieve better results if you first wet the DAS, as the wire brush will add more texture if slightly wet. It is well worth practising this skill as small sections of exposed stonework add much character and interest to model buildings.

Looking back at this feature I should have sculpted a more haphazard design rather than keeping to a formal straight edge and level design of stonework.

This stonework was further textured by adding a layer of texturing medium—acrylic gel with fine powder added. I stipple this medium onto the stonework with a stiff brush or use a detail brush to pick out individual stones. The effect can only be seen when painted and, in particular, when drybrushed.

The Roof

The article in the Almark book showed how the roof tiles could be constructed from thin plastic card, cut into rectangles with the lower edges trimmed off before adding them one at a time to the sloped roofs. I chose the same technique with one exception: I chose card rather than plastic card.

I marked out a piece of 0.75mm thick card – the backing card from an A3 sketch pad into rectangles 12mm long by 8mm wide. I then cut out enough to cover the model roofs and while sitting in the living room, with one eye on the TV, I proceeded to apply over 500 individual roof tiles. I used PVA glue to apply them but only after I had trimmed the lower edges of each tile with nail scissors – as featured in the original articles.

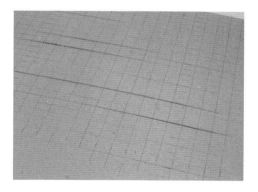

At this stage, I feel I should point out to anyone new to building a roof with individual tiles that this is not a quick fix—in fact it is mind-numbing, but I have yet to find a better way of

tiling roofs. I start by adding a longitudinal strip across the bottom of the roof—I do this to stop the lower tiles from lying at a different angle to the rest of the roof. Once this is in place I start at the lower edge (usually the left corner) and build up the roof in regular layers. It is sometimes said that you should add lots of damaged or out-of-place tiles to the roof, but I have always been under the impression that with very few exceptions most tiled roofs are very well cared for.

The tiling is best done in one sitting as you can get variations in the spacing if you try to do it over two or more sittings.

I also add 'hills and valleys' to my roofs. To do this, I add thin (or thick) strips of paper or card up the roof and over the roof ridge. These strips give a slight undulation effect to the underlying structure which, when tiled with the individual tiles, gives a subtle ripple effect to the roof. Try not to be too heavy-handed—subtle is better.

The final run of tiles – the ridge tiles can be modelled in many different forms – I prefer to have the tiles butt joined on the ridge and I add a strip of DAS to the very top to mimic cement or lime plaster. The same DAS is also used to add cement to any joins between tiles and tiles or tiles and wall.

With the roof fully modelled I find that a layer of dilute PVA glue helps to secure everything in place.

After drying the whole roof with a hairdryer (one of my most often used tools), I then add some subtle texture to the roof. In this case a mix of water, PVA glue, acrylic medium, ground stone (powder) and even sawdust is scrubbed or stippled on to the roof tiles. You may have to do this two or three times to get the right effect, but it is worth the effort when painted. The PVA glue and medium mix also helps to harden up the card.

If you copy this technique, you should now have a beautifully modelled tiled roof with a slight texture as seen on real tiled roofs.

I also like to use a less textured medium and/
or a fine powder mix to the plain walls, while
the groundwork is more heavily textured
in distinct layers with first small stones or
sieved stones, then coarse sand and finally
fine sand. I know that some modellers add
this texturing in one layer – mixing the three
grades of texture together. I find that you get
better control if these layers are separate and applied one after the other.

These images show most of the main construction and I have tried to write in detail
about each individual step. Even so there are lots of additional details that have been added
– for example small cracks in the plaster walls, a resin barrel to the rear and slight curves
sanded into the surface of the steps to show wear and tear. However with the chimney pot
added, the construction is now complete.

Painting

I started with an all-over undercoat/
basecoat of Titanium White. I wanted
to paint this model in a different
colour from my usual ochre or cream
and so chose a soft pink colour that I
had seen in a book on regional French
architecture as inspiration. The first
colour was a terracotta red/orange that
looks very similar to the DAS terracotta
clay that was used to model this house.

A first highlight used Ochre and red to tone down the terracotta. This was painted on with a large hogs-hair brush using a stippling action.

The second highlight used a very soft pink/white which was drybrushed across the surface of the model but allowing the earlier base colours to show through.

The third highlight used more cream and white to pick out the sculpted detail.

Prior to adding the next highlight, I painted the exposed stonework in grey/pale brown and white. Notice how I have allowed the earlier colours to remain in the recessed areas of the house.

I used a stiff Daler Bristlewhite brush for the highlighting or drybrushing of the stonework.

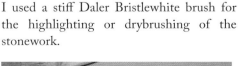

The next step was to add some colour to the architectural stonework and using a smaller No 3 detail brush and watered-down acrylic paint, so I base-coated these features in a variety of natural colours.

The rear of the house was painted in the same way – I have left the darker or base colours to show through along the bottom of the walls. Another lighter drybrush and the walls are nearly finished.

The next step was to paint the groundwork and for this it was back to my trusty Snakebite Leather from Games Workshop. I have used a large brush, watered down the paint and applied two good layers.

The Roof

The roof was undercoated with a medium to dark grey basecoat as I wanted to portray a slate roof. Odd tiles were picked out in darker and different colours.

Then the roof was drybrushed with a lighter grey.

The wooden roof supports and windows were painted in a green/brown mix that was purposely mixed on both the palette and the model as I wanted a slightly run-down and worn look.

The tiled roof, wooden areas and groundwork were once again highlighted with both drybrushing and detail painting before the painting was finished.

I have added grey coloured fillets around the chimney and roof joins, the small items of clutter have been painted and the wooden barrel and wood stack have been base-coated, highlighted and drybrushed.

The lower area of the wall (where it meets with the groundwork) has been washed with various browns to blend the walls into the base. I wet the area with what I call 'wet-water' (water to which I have added some washing up liquid) and then apply watered-down washes with a large watercolour brush. If you find that you have added too much paint or colour, just wash with more water.

Detailing

Before I varnished the model, I have added lots of detail painting to the roof (mould and lichen stains), the doors and woodwork (nails and rust) and the groundwork (small stones and rocks).

The glazed parts of the windows have been painted with a watered-down black/blue paint, with a darker lower right and a lighter upper left – this, I think gives a very good impression of glazed windows.

After varnishing with Galleria Matt Varnish, I painted the glazed windows with Future Floor Polish (an acrylic gloss polish/varnish) then added some dyed sawdust over PVA glue and some static grass tufts (with superglue). As you can see, I have now given this house a name—Le Rose—which was painted on with a fine brush and watered-down acrylic paint. The two storey French house shows how I build my replicas with DAS modelling clay over

corrugated cardboard and balsa wood, how the walls and details can be built up in layers and then, when needed, carved back to show exposed stonework. It also demonstrates how the DAS can be sculpted and textured to produce a huge range of different surface effects. DAS is one of my favourite modelling mediums.

The model measures 190mm long x 80mm wide x 120mm tall. The plastic card base is 220 x 160mm.

Materials Used
- Corrugated cardboard
- Card
- Balsa wood
- Green foam
- DAS modelling clay—Terracotta and White

- Plastic card
- Plastic rod
- Resin castings
- Florists' wire
- Artists' modelling paste
- Fine sand and sieved stones
- Dyed sawdust
- Ground foam
- Static grass

Paints used
- Titanium White tube acrylic
- Terracotta craft paint
- Cream craft paint
- Linen craft paint
- Citadel Snakebite Leather/Leather Brown
- Dead White
- Stonewall Grey
- Goblin Green
- Dark Green
- Magic Blue
- Charred Brown
- Gory Red
- Bloody Red
- Hot Orange
- Black
- Various washes—both bought and home-made.
- Galleria matt varnish
- Future floor polish (gloss varnish)

20mm
LA BELLE
ALLIANCE

A'LA BELLE
ALLIANCE &
WELLINGTON
HOTEL

1.3

20MM LA BELLE ALLIANCE

TARTING-UP MDF LASER-CUT BUILDING KITS

Inspiration

Some years ago I scratch-built a master model of La Belle Alliance – a model that was originally planned as a 28mm resin casting, but due to various constraints, the model was never made available commercially. In planning for this model I produced detailed 28mm or 1/56th scale plans which have remained unused and stored in the garage.

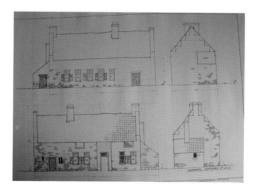

Skip forward to January 2017 and I saw that a model of La Belle was now available as a 20mm MDF or laser cut kit from Sarissa Precision so I thought I would produce a model of this iconic Napoleonic building using this kit but also show how I would modify it or customise it so it was a more accurate representation of this famous building.

I am not a great fan of MDF kits as I find them too flat and way too simplistic; however, I have written magazine articles in the past showing how these kits can be improved. These articles proved to be very popular and by including this building in this book, I can show a building in a different scale as well as offering hints on how to improve these 'wooden' kits. The term 'tarting-up MDF' was originally coined by Guy Bowers, the editor of *Wargames, Soldiers and Strategy* magazine for a short series of construction articles I wrote in 2016.

The model was purchased from Sarissa for £16.00, plus postage.

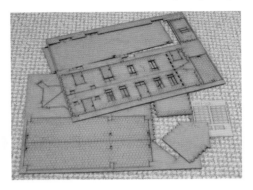

Illustrations of La Belle Alliance show the building with a pantiled roof (sometimes heavily damaged). I purchased a set of Wills-Ratio plastic card pantile roof (SSMP206) to replace the laser-cut roof sections supplied with the kit as well as a set of cobblestone walling (SSMP205) to decorate the base. Wills kits are intended for the railway modeller and are scaled at 'OO' (3.5mm = 1 foot) which makes them a little too small for 1/56th scale or 28mm figures, but ideal for 20mm gaming miniatures.

The Wills kits cost £3.18 for the pantiles and £2.25 for the cobblestone walling. Similar kits are available from various suppliers via the internet or at shows.

Studying various images of this historic building and reverting back to my own scale drawings, I noticed two inaccuracies with the laser-cut kit: firstly, the walls are not tall enough—I estimate that the front and rear walls should be at least 8mm taller; and secondly, the outbuilding to the right should be stone built and narrower than the main building. It is my intention to modify the original kit to correct these faults.

The walls of the Sarissa kit are just 2mm thick and I think it would be a good idea to add an inner false wall or clad the main walls on the inside to make the structure stronger.

Construction
My first job was to add a strip of MDF to the tops of the front and back walls. In the end

I used strips 11mm tall which is slightly higher than I had first planned.

These strips were added to backing card made from 60mm tall art board and glued to the lower wall and the extension with superglue. This had the added advantages of acting as a support for the upper extension, a backing to the laser cut windows and thickening up the rather thin 2mm thick MDF of the kit.

On the rear of the building I filled in the two upper storey windows with small off-cuts of MDF and recut them in the raised extension.

I glued the two gable ends into place with superglue, raising them to fit with the top of the side walls and leaving an 11mm gap towards the bottom.

With the four main walls of the structure in place, I added internal support walls to each end. These support walls were constructed from more art board.

Before the four walls were glued to the supplied MDF base, I added the two 11mm tall fillers to the bottom of the gable ends and trimmed the lean-to extension so that it no longer went all the way across the end, but only 48mm along the wall. This meant modifying the end wall to fit and I took the opportunity to reduce the two windows of the kit to one window as well as making this one window slightly smaller.

The MDF base has been trimmed back along the front edge, but left untouched along the rear.

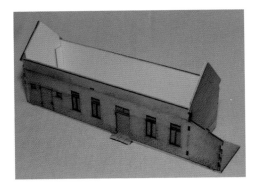 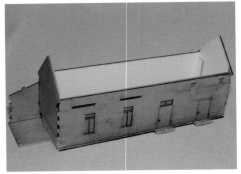

The slope of the lean-to roof is a little too shallow so I added another internal support from art board and increased the slope to be more in keeping with my plans.

At this stage the modifications have made the model look more like some of the contemporary illustrations, but I now think that the building looks too thin and that it should be about 10mm deeper from front to back. Given the number of modifications I have already made, I think I will leave the width as it is rather than try to cut the model apart and increase it.

The MDF lean-to roof was trimmed to size and glued in place with superglue.

Now I have started to add some of the modifications I had illustrated on my initial plans. I have used 0.75mm thick card to add an extended panel above and around the main door as well as a new door frame. You can see that I have removed the original main door, as this should be panelled and not planked as included in the Sarissa kit. I will add the new scratch-built door later.

The lean-to extension to the side of the main building should be built of exposed stone and to model this I have carved the stone courses with a new scalpel. I start by marking in some horizontal cuts (try not to make them too level) and then the vertical cuts. Once they are done, I go over the stone effect with a small wire brush. To achieve this effect, you may need to go over the area a couple of times before you have the finish you want.

Detailing

The front of this building is pictured in many contemporary images as having a more solid framing around the four main windows. I used some thin card (the cardboard from a toothpaste carton) to mark out and then cut out four new frames. These were glued in place with superglue. In addition there were two additions above these windows—one to either side of the main door. I cannot be certain, but these look like bricked-in dormer windows. In fact I would hazard a guess that La Belle Alliance once had a thatched roof with two dormers. When the building was re-roofed with tiles, I believe that the dormers were filled in. I also believe that the gable ends were re-built from a 'stepped end' to a sloped end, as there are triangles of infill seen on many images of this building. I would hope to be able to replicate these triangles or infills when painting the model.

I am convinced that the building went through at least three and possibly four building phases. 1—a shorter, thatched building; 2—re-roofed with a tiled roof and the dormer windows filled in; 3—an extended or longer building with the first extension to the left (as you look at the front; 4—a smaller, stone built lean-to extension to the right.

La Belle Alliance is still standing, but the thing about researching these buildings is that you can never be 100 per cent sure just what they actually looked like during the Napoleonic Wars as a lot of the published images were made after (sometimes long after) the battle.

I have used DAS modelling clay and acrylic modelling paste both to cover up the joins and add texture to the surfaces of the building. This was done in two or three sessions, as I believe it better to build up this texture a bit at a time rather than trying to get it right in one go.

The kit roof was trimmed back to fit inside the gable ends and not overlap the front and back walls. The MDF panels were glued in place over internal supports with superglue and any gaps were filled with DAS—remember, I will be retiling the roof with the Wills plastic card Pantiles.

The gable ends were extended with some off-cuts of green foam. I trimmed the foam to a rough fit and superglued two strips to each end. When the superglue was fully set,

I trimmed back the foam and then sanded the surfaces smooth. To make sure I had hidden any joins, I painted on some acrylic modelling paste to which I had added some fine modelling powder. Any obvious joins were filled with DAS.

At this stage of construction, you could be forgiven for asking why I had not scratch built the whole building. I am asking myself the same question. I don't think there is a square centimetre that has not been modified or customised or textured! Still, I'm enjoying detailing this simple kit.

The (Pantile) Roof

I then built the right-hand chimney from an off-cut of green foam. It was a simple matter of producing a rectangular block and cutting an inverted 'V' into the bottom before gluing in place with superglue (see below). A finial was placed on the left hand gable end and again, this was constructed from green foam. Any gaps were filled and smoothed over with DAS before I painted on a filler/PVA glue mix to seal the foam.

The pantile roof on the stone built extension was cut from the Wills-Ratio Pantile set and glued in place with superglue. The small chimney sticking through the roof was made from a strip of balsa wood and detailed with card. The cement in-fill (where the tiles meet the chimney and wall) was sculpted from DAS.

I found the Wills-Ratio plastic very difficult to cut. I scored the card with a scalpel and then snapped it to size. I sanded and trimmed the edges to give them a little more definition. If you study the gable ends, you can see how I have added small cut-out detail to the upper gable ends in the shape of small triangles as seen on my plans and many contemporary images.

The sign on the left hand gable was constructed from card and glued in place with superglue. I have to admit that I have some doubts as to whether this sign was in place at the time of the Battle of Waterloo—I think it was a later addition. However I have decided to include it. A little bit of artistic licence.

One of my main complaints about MDF or laser-cut buildings is the roofs. In most instances, they are a flat piece of MDF with the tile pattern burnt in. I feel that this is simple to fix by either cladding with roof panels (as I am doing) or adding individual tiles as seen in earlier tutorials. The roofs of our terrain pieces are some of the more obvious items on a wargames table and any improvements will be seen to be worth it, especially when painted and detailed.

The main roof sections were a little easier to both cut and fit than the small roof on the lean-to. The front of the building uses three trimmed sections of the Wills pantile roofing, while the rear uses two. I first sanded the lower edges with a sanding stick and then scored the plastic card to a height of

13 tiles. The plastic card pantile panels were glued in place with superglue and accelerator. It was easier than I had anticipated to get the roof sections to line up with one another, although there will still be some filling.

The central chimney is shown on most of the contemporary images as being about twice as large as the chimney to the right.

Once again it was constructed from green foam with some thin card detailing. The inverted 'V' was cut into the bottom and the chimney was glued in place with superglue.

The cement fillets around the chimney and against the internal gable ends were originally planned to be Milliput, but in the end, I choose to use DAS. The fillet along the top of the roof is also DAS, applied over PVA glue and sculpted to shape with the point of a dental tool. Once the sculpting was done, I 'feathered' out the edges and softened the DAS by painting on some dilute PVA glue.

When you look along the Wills-Ratio pantile tiles, there is just the right amount of ripple to make it look authentic in 20mm, although I'm not sure I will be using them again as they look much too small in my preferred 28mm-30mm scale.

Finishing off the detailing

I decided to use just five of the cut card window shutters and even these were cut down from the original ones in the kit. I choose to do this as images on the internet show some missing and only covering the lower, rather than the upper *and* lower windows. These shutters, although a small detail, do add to the authentic effect I was looking for. The hinges for the shutters are just small slivers of card glued in place with PVA glue.

I chose not to have any shutters on the rear of the building for the main reason that I was not sure there were any.

The main door was constructed from two pieces of card again glued together and in place with PVA glue. The door knobs are sections of plastic rod.

I have used finely textured acrylic paint to add some more surface detail to the chimneys and some of the wall sections. I am still undecided as to whether I will add a base to this model. I am thinking of gluing it to a small diorama base.

In some of these images, you might wonder why there are red marks on the model's surfaces. I do most of my model-making in the shed at the bottom of the garden and take photos in my computer room/spare bedroom. I find that when the images are studied on the computer, I see small errors that need to be corrected and marking them in red makes sure that I don't miss them when I get back to the shed!

I have decided to mount the model on to a base. I have used a piece of 3mm thick plastic card which was cut into a rectangle of 6 inches x 12 inches. The MDF building was positioned centrally, with the main walls running along the longer axis. I used a latex cobblestone textured base as a decorative feature and built up the rest of the base with DAS modelling clay.

Once the DAS was set, I added some sieved stones and fine sand to further texture the groundwork. I further sealed the groundwork by coating it with some dilute PVA glue.

Painting

I have started with the pantile roof. The first colours were Leather Brown, German Orange and Yellow Ochre. The colours were applied with a large brush and mixed on the roof surface. This base colour was added to with Beastly Brown and Chocolate Brown, picking up odd tiles and working around the base of the

chimneys. This first highlight was mixed from the same colours but with some Buff and White Grey.

The roof was then drybrushed with a Buff and Dead White before individual tiles were picked out in various colours as detailed above. One more drybrush with Buff and Dead White and then another bash at picking out some darker tiles, this time with Charred Brown and Black.

Just prior to taking this image, I gave the whole roof a light 'wash' of dirty water— literally the water from my mixing pot.

The stone built extension to the right was painted to represent grey stone. The first base colour was a Black, Buff and Dead White mix, but with some Leather Brown added to the lower wall areas. The drybrushing was more Black and Dead White before I washed the area with some dirty water.

The windows were painted in a dark grey, mid grey, light grey pattern which was mixed from Black and Dead White. It was a new technique for me, with the darker grey to the bottom right and the lighter grey to the top left. I have also tinted the lower wall on the stone built extension. I had seen on some images of this building that the stonework varied from grey to brown on this section and I thought I would try to replicate this.

I have tried to replicate the colours shown in a pair of images of La Belle Alliance, a sort of cream, grey ochre that is mottled across the entire surface and with a grey or greyer colour to the lower edges.

The whitewashed areas around the doors and windows were next. I have used two greys, Stonewall Grey and White Grey as well as Dead White to build up the white areas in three stages. In truth, I think the white is a little too stark, but I can always tone this down later with a wash.

The cobbled areas of the base were painted grey, mixed from Black and Dead White. The highlights were mixed with more white in the mix.

The shutters and doors have been painted brown.

I used my tried and trusted colour choice for the groundwork—Snakebite Leather from Games Workshop, highlighted with Snakebite and white with odd stones picked out in grey, highlighted white and then washed with earth and sepia washes.

Prior to varnishing the whole model with Galleria matt varnish, I touched up any areas of over-painting and covered a couple of areas with various washes.

The signs were painted in dark grey over pencil guides following the design featured on the prints mentioned earlier.

The groundwork has been further detailed by adding some static grass, static grass tufts and ground foam.

Conclusion

Although the model was a fun build and one that I enjoyed slotting together and painting, my views about laser-cut MDF have not changed. I still don't like the material or the rather 'flat' finish they produce. However, I am pleased with the finished model and believe it to be a very good representation of this famous building. The use of the Wills Pantile plastic roof sheets has helped to add some much needed surface texture to the model.

The model is 250mm long x 70mm deep and 115mm tall (to the top of the larger chimney), It is mounted on a plastic card base 300mm x 150mm.

Materials Used

- Sarissa Precision Waterloo La Belle Alliance kit (H203) 20mm scale
- DAS modelling clay
- Green foam
- Balsa wood
- Card/art board
- Wills pantile roof tiles (SSMP206)
- Latex cobble stone base
- Plastic card
- Plastic rod
- Acrylic modelling paste
- Sand and sieved stones

Paints Used

- Titanium White tube acrylic paint
- Leather Brown
- German Grey
- Hot Orange
- Yellow Ochre
- Beastly Brown
- Chocolate Brown
- Buff
- White Grey
- Linen
- Dead White
- Charred Brown
- Black
- Stonewall Grey
- White Grey
- Snakebite Leather
- White Grey (VMC 70.993)
- Sepia Wash (Games Workshop)
- Black Wash (Games Workshop)

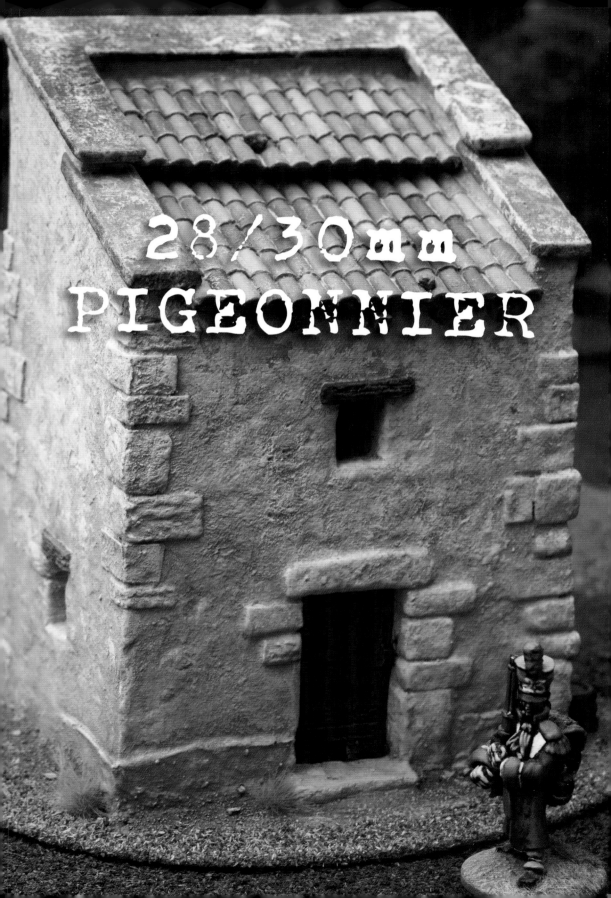

28/30mm
PIGEONNIER

2.1
28/30MM PIGEONNIER

A RURAL FRENCH DOVECOTE

Following on from the La Belle Alliance MDF model, I needed to build something that better suited my modelling style, more rustic and with fewer straight lines! This rural *pigeonnier* was just what I needed.

Inspiration

The dovecote is modelled on a couple of different dovecotes. One in particular, from page 102 in the book *The French Farmhouse* by Elsie Burch Donald was used as the basis of the initial plan. The pale, parched colours were copied from the same book. I sketched a simple structure based not on any one dovecote, but more an amalgamation of a couple of examples from Southern France. I have read that at their height, there were over 42,000 dovecotes in France, ranging from the simple to the elaborate as only the French can imagine.

The basic core was once again cut from scrap corrugated cardboard.

The cardboard was glued together with my hot glue gun.

The core was strengthened with strips of torn newspaper glued in place and further coated with dilute PVA glue. This core would act as a base on which further detail could be sculpted with DAS modelling clay.

I realised quite quickly that the upper walls would have to be extended and I did this with some strips of green foam which was glued in place with superglue. The joins and edges were further detailed with DAS modelling clay.

My next step was to start work on the walls. I like DAS modelling clay as it is easy and clean to use and if you dry it in the oven, construction moves along very quickly. However, it is easy to have walls that have too smooth a finish and this was not an effect I was looking for. I wanted an uneven and rickety wall, with the underlying stones showing through in places. To replicate this, I added green foam laminations to the walls, particularly around the door and window openings and up the sides or corners of the walls. These stones will be covered with DAS or filler and don't have to be too detailed—think of them as a substructure. You can see in this image that I have used both terracotta DAS and white DAS.

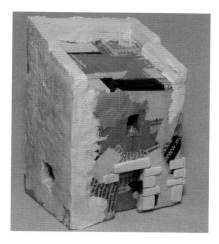

More DAS, and I hope you can see that the walls are not perpendicular, but slope inwards as they rise. This was a feature I had seen on many rustic buildings and something I wanted to replicate on this model.

I think it is fair to say that the model does not look like much at these early stages!

My next step was to add a base. I think it is the right time to say that I prefer building models with bases rather than those that have none. I like the presence of a base, I think it adds to, rather than takes away from the model, and it gives me the opportunity to 'bed' the model into its foundations as well as add clutter. I have nothing against models without bases, nor do I feel that all models should have bases; I just prefer bases on my models. And my bases of choice are made from thick plastic card (actually ex-advertising signs).

The *pigeonnier* is based on a rough oval of 3mm thick plastic card that has had the edges chamfered and sanded. You can see that the dovecote is not attached directly to the plastic card base, but has a spacer of more plastic card between the model and the base. This is something I do on the majority of my scratch-built terrain as I think it helps with the 'bedding-in' of the model and forces me to add more body to my groundwork.

The dovecote with base was glued onto the plastic card base with superglue.

The lower walls were built up with more DAS. You should also see that I have added a small ridge to the lower wall, a feature I first saw on some Snapdragon resin buildings and something that I add to many of my own structures.

 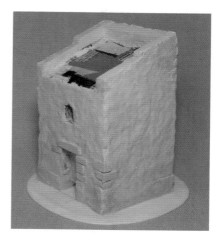

The groundwork and threshold was built from DAS applied over PVA glue. I should also add that I like to score my plastic card bases to help the DAS and glue adhere.

The Roof

I wanted to model a clay tile roof, sometimes called a canal tile or Roman tile. I have, in the past, scratch-built my own canal tile roofs from beads, corduroy and plastic tubes, but actually find it much easier and quicker to buy some ready-made tile roof sections. These resin roof sections were bought on the internet after seeing them advertised on *The Lead Adventure* forum. I have had them in my spares box for some time and I thought I would use them here.

The roof tile section had the base sanded smooth and was then glued in place with superglue.

The lower edges were detailed by engraving the hollow tile profiles with a fine drill bit in my Dremel. The exposed wooden supports were constructed from some thick plastic card and glued in place with superglue.

In addition, I have extended the lower roof sections by adding a layer of capping stones. These capping stones were constructed from green foam and detailed with DAS.

The upper roof was built in the same way.

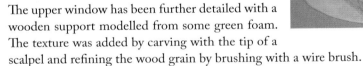

The upper window has been further detailed with a wooden support modelled from some green foam. The texture was added by carving with the tip of a scalpel and refining the wood grain by brushing with a wire brush.

The exposed stones in the wall have been further refined and additional corner stones added by gluing thin veneers of green foam over superglue and then texturing the green foam with a fine filler and PVA glue mix.

These additional surface stones have also been added to the rear.

The canal tiled roof had additional texture added by carving out the odd canal tile and chipping the edges of some exposed tiles with the tip of a scalpel. I have also painted on some fine grit applied over PVA glue and glued in place a

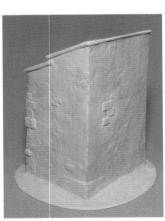

couple of larger stones. These ballast stones were regularly placed on canal tile roofs to stop them coming loose in high winds.

The groundwork was textured by applying PVA glue in sections and sprinkling on some sieved stones, sand and fine sand, then adding some 'wet water' (water to which a small drop of washing-up liquid has been added which helps to break the surface tension) to allow the glue to grip the sand.

Additional texturing has been added to some of the exposed stones in the walls—you should be able to see it as a whiter texturing.

The main door was constructed from small off-cuts of green foam (never throw anything away!) and a small resin barrel has been added to the right hand side of the base.

Painting

I gave the whole model a quick undercoat of diluted acrylic white paint and then tried a new basecoat technique. I washed the whole building, walls, tiled roof and base with some diluted Umber tube acrylic paint which was painted on with a large flat-head brush.

This was then over-painted with some Linen which was scrubbed onto the walls with an old brush. I have tried to keep the darker Umber colour to the base and a much lighter almost pure white colour for the upper walls or highlights. A quick wash of dirty water—literally the dirty water from my paint brush cleaning jar—and I had the start of a natural looking pale cream wall colour. I scrubbed the upper wall area with some more off-white and the main walls were done.

The woodwork areas were painted a dirty brown-grey and highlighted with some more grey to show old and dried-out, untreated wood.

I then started the fun job of painting the individual canal tiles one by one. I used a mixed palette of orange, red, brown and cream and mixed each tile colour on the palette before painting the tiles. I find that diluting the paint makes it easier to apply.

I like to paint the tiles one at a time and leave small areas of the cream or white undercoat showing through as this looks like concrete or cement at the joins—don't forget to paint the ends of the lower tiles.

The canal tiles were drybrushed with a lighter cream colour—this is to highlight the edges and helps to make the different coloured tiles blend in. The three ballast stones were painted in tones of grey.

The upper roof area was painted in a slightly different colour, a grey/cream that was similar to the wall colour but with some black and white added. These areas were then stippled with some lighter mid- and topcoats before the whole model was once again given a wash of dirty water.

I painted the base in my usual Snakebite Leather with darker brown nearer to the walls and a Snakebite/Skull White to the edges. When this was fully dry, I highlighted the groundwork with more white added to the mix and then picked out individual stones in grey highlighted with white.

The lower wall and groundwork area was blended in by applying a wash of 'wet water' and then adding various washes of brown and black. I find that this application of washes helps to hide any stark border between wall and groundwork. I try to have a gradual blending from the Snakebite colour of the ground to the pale Linen of the walls, while still accentuating any sculpted detail.

The small wooden barrel to the side was painted in muted browns with black banding.

Prior to varnishing, I added one more wash of dirty water to the canal tiles and the wooden roof supports.

The base is decorated with dyed sawdust applied over PVA glue and a couple of clumps of static grass tufts which were glued in place with superglue.

The model didn't take that long to build and the use of watered-down washes to paint the walls meant that the completed dovecote took less time from start to finish than any of the other models in this book. The resin cast canal tiles were a lot easier and quicker to use than scratch-building each one.

The model is 95mm x 80mm x 140mm tall and it is mounted on a 3mm thick plastic card base which measures 140mm x 130mm.

Materials used
- Corrugated cardboard
- Card
- Resin cast canal tiles purchased via *The Lead Adventure Forum*
- Green foam
- Plastic card
- Sieved stones and fine sand
- Acrylic modelling paste
- DAS modelling clay
- Resin barrel
- Balsa wood

Paints used
- Titanium White tube acrylic
- Umber tube acrylic
- Burnt Umber
- Dead White
- Cream
- Stonewall Grey
- Barbarian Leather
- Charred Brown
- Black
- Hot Orange
- Sun Yellow
- Bloody Red
- Snakebite Leather
- Games Workshop and Vallejo washes
- Galleria matt varnish

28/30mm
STONE
BUILT WELL

2.2
28/30MM STONE BUILT WELL

BUILDING A STONE STRUCTURE STONE-BY-STONE

Inspiration

The 2011 film *Red Riding Hood* was the inspiration for this small piece. I saw the rough stone well when watching it on TV and thought that it would make a great little model. I did a couple of quick sketches while watching the film and then searched the internet for more. The film set is built around a town square in the centre of which is a low stone well built, like some of the other structures, from large, flat stones. I would suggest that the building style is Eastern European or 'fairy tale' and therefore fits in with buildings that featured in the Russian campaign.

I have to admit that there were quite a few buildings that could have been the inspiration for models, but the well was so unusual in its construction that I thought it was worth including. The well was built at the same time as the French dovecote.

Construction

My first job was to make some stones from green foam. These were cut from thin slices of foam, trimmed to shape and then sanded with a sanding stick, before I impressed some stone texture into the foam by pressing some rough stones on the surface. The stones used were a broken tile (one of my favourite tools for adding texture), a large stone from the garden and the sharp edge of a piece of scrap slate.

I modelled about 40 stones before I started construction on the rectangular well.

The base was cut from some 3mm thick plastic card (ex-advertising sign) with the edges first trimmed and then sanded smooth. The first layer was some thick card, which I will clad with foam stones later.

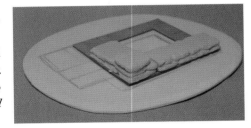

Then layers or courses of foam stones are glued in place with superglue.

As the walls of the well grew, I defined some of the edges with DAS modelling clay. I wanted a rectangular shape, but not too regular a shape as the initial *Red Riding Hood* well had looked very rustic.

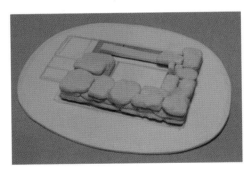

More layers are added. With the basic shape now finished, I textured the stones with some dilute filler to which I had added some fine marble dust which is sold as a filler or additive for acrylic paints.

The groundwork was built with DAS modelling clay applied over PVA glue. When applying the DAS to the plastic card, I like to 'score' the plastic card surface with a scalpel as I believe that this helps the DAS to stick and reduces the chance of it breaking off or shrinking.

I had noticed that the well shown on the film set had some odd or loose stones scattered around the base. I reproduced this by adding a couple of spare green foam stones to the groundwork. These were cut at an angle and embedded into the DAS.

The well's winding structure was inspired by a different well, this one seen on the internet which had a large wooden wheel that was used to turn the axle and lift the bucket.

The uprights were built from a couple of off-cuts of modelling foam, while the wheel was cut from another piece of foam, textured with a scalpel and brushed with a wire brush. The axle was a bamboo barbecue skewer and the rest of the bits were salvaged from my 'bits box'.

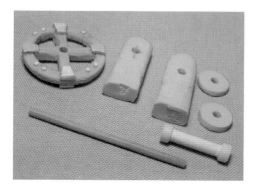

I mounted the stone uprights into the well base, cutting out a couple of stones before gluing them in place with superglue. I then used foam and DAS modelling clay to remodel the walls of the well.

The wheel was detailed with some slivers of plastic rod and some thin balsa wood supports.

Once again I used sieved stones and sand to texture the groundwork. I applied some dilute PVA glue to the DAS modelling clay then sprinkled on some sieved stones, rough sand and then fine sand before flooding the area with very dilute PVA glue, to which I have added some washing up liquid. This 'wet water' seeps through the PVA glue and the stones and when fully dry gives a very tough and textured surface.

Painting
As usual I gave the whole model a rough undercoat of dark brown, which was mixed from Charred Brown and Black.

I then painted on a mid-grey first coat. This first coat is only a base coat and is usually applied quite roughly. The detail painting will come later.

The next layer is more of a drybrush and highlights the texture of the individual stones. The groundwork has been given a couple of coats of dilute Snakebite Leather. I prefer to build up these colours with dilute paint as I find that it does not hide the sculpted texture.

The Snakebite undercoated groundwork is further highlighted with a drybrushing of Snakebite and white.

Then individual stones are picked out in grey. I start by painting odd stones with watered-down dark grey, then highlighting with mid grey and finally further highlighting with a near pure white.

The wheel was pressed in place (not glued), then given another drybrush.

Now I painted the water. I started with a black/blue, then highlighted with a dark blue then further highlighted with Regal Blue, finishing off with a Regal Blue/white highlight.

For the well rope, I used some Christmas tag thread that, although over-scale, had a pronounced twisted texture that I believed would look good painted. The water bucket was a resin barrel casting that was initially intended as a ship's fitting. The handle was modelled from florists' wire and some slivers of plastic rod.

The rope and bucket were painted with acrylic paints and glued in place with superglue.

I used sandpaper to rub down a coloured chalk and then applied this dust to the stonework. The effect is subtle, but does add a slight coloured tint to the otherwise plain grey stones. In addition, I have used washes to tint the upper surface of the stone well.

The model was been varnished with Galleria Matt Varnish, after which I applied some gloss varnish to the barrel, rope and upper stones.

The water in the bottom of the well was also gloss varnished, whilst the base was decorated with dyed sawdust, static grass and static grass tufts.

This small model was great fun to make and the techniques used to build up a stone structure from individual foam stones could be used in many different models.

The well is not large, just 105mm x 70mm x 48mm tall (to the top of the wooden wheel/winch). It is mounted on a 3mm thick plastic card base which measures 150mm x 130mm.

Materials used
- Green foam
- Card
- Plastic card
- Plastic rod
- Orange foam
- Balsa wood
- Plastic pen barrel
- Knitting needle
- Christmas decoration thread
- Resin barrel
- Florists wire
- Bamboo skewer
- Coloured chalk

Paints used
- Black
- Charred Brown
- Stonewall Grey
- White
- Barbarian Leather
- Dark Blue
- Regal Blue
- Green
- Citadel and Vallejo washes
- Galleria matt varnish
- Homebase gloss varnish

28/30mm
RUSSIAN
GRANARY

2.3
28/30MM RUSSIAN GRANARY

WORKING WITH BALSA WOOD

Inspiration

Like the earlier tutorial for the Russian windmill, the inspiration for this particular model was found in the book *Architecture of the Russian North*. Towards the back of the book, on pages 193 and 194, are a couple of full-colour images of wooden or log-built grain stores, simple log structures mounted on wooden supports to house grain for the winter. I had wanted to model one of these structures for some time and feel that the techniques shown in this tutorial could be of use to many modellers when building log cabins.

As with most of my scratch-built projects, it started with a simple sketch.

Construction

Corrugated cardboard profiles were cut out.

These were then glued together with my hot glue gun to form a simple cube. This simple former was clad with more corrugated cardboard onto which I will add textured balsa wood.

I have used balsa wood to model the wooden posts or logs that are interlocked around the basic structure. The balsa wood was given to me by my sister-in-law's father. Thank you Alex. After texturing the logs with coarse sandpaper, I used superglue to glue the balsa wood into place.

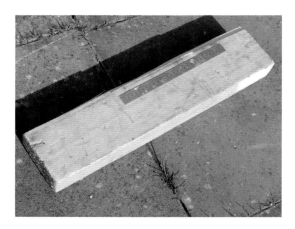

The model is shown alongside the colour image in the book *Architecture of the Russian North*.

More textured balsa wood and the simple granary begins to take shape. The lengths of balsa wood were notched on the ends so that they could interlock with one another. The cladding continued until the whole building was covered.

More balsa wood and the roof support and upper front were clad. Once again I used superglue.

The detailing on the wooden roof was done with both balsa wood and some thin veneer. I have also used green foam to model some of the protruding beams. DAS modelling clay was used as a filler.

On the rear wall, I wanted to replicate the exposed log ends, so carved and sanded some green foam into long cylinders then cut them to size before gluing them into place below the eaves.

The platform was also modelled from balsa wood. Detailing on the door was modelled from plastic card and plastic rod.

The wooden mushroom legs or supports were also built from balsa wood. These were glued in place with more superglue.

Each mushroom was modelled from two sections of balsa wood then glued to the base of the platform.

As with all of my terrain models, I have mounted the Granary on to a piece of 3mm plastic card. The card has been detailed with DAS modelling clay applied over PVA glue. At this moment the platform and granary have the mushroom supports glued in place, but the supports are not glued to the plastic card/DAS base.

Detailing

The DAS groundwork was further textured with sieved stones and sand, applied over PVA glue. The grain sacks resting on the platform were sculpted from even more DAS and I have used small slivers of plastic card and plastic rod to add nails to the wooden roof and door.

Painting

The granary was base-coated/undercoated with a very dark black/brown mix that was slapped on with a large hog's hair brush, while the groundwork was painted with a Snakebite Leather colour.

Initial drybrushing was done by adding white or light grey to the mix. This drybrushing picked out the surface detail, and was followed by yet another drybrushing.

The groundwork has been painted as earlier tutorials, drybrushing and picking out odd stones, while the main structure has now been given a number of watered down washes to highlight different colours in the aged wood.

At this stage, the granary and base are still not attached. I thought this would make painting and detailing a little easier.

Prior to varnishing with Galleria matt varnish, I painted the three sacks of grain, detailed the metalwork on the door and highlighted the nails. I used superglue to join the granary to the base, which was then decorated with dyed sawdust and odd tufts of static grass.

The granary is a small model just 80mm wide x 80mm deep and 100mm tall. It is mounted on to a 3mm thick plastic card base that is 110mm x 120mm.

Although a simple structure, I believe that the techniques used could be used to build a larger log structure for use in a number of different genres.

Materials used
* Corrugated card
* Card
* Balsa wood
* Green foam
* Scrap wood
* Plastic card
* Plastic rod
* DAS modelling clay

Paints used
* Black
* Charred Brown
* Barbarian Brown
* White
* Stonewall Grey
* Hot Orange
* Snakebite Leather
* Linen
* Forest Green
* Games Workshop and Vallejo washes
* Galleria matt varnish

28/30mm
DIE KLEINE
BÄCKEREI

3.1
28/30MM DIE KLEINE BÄCKEREI

THE SMALL BAKERY

Inspiration

This model is based on a Lilliput Lane[1] sculpt called *Die Kleine Bäckerei or The Small Bakery* from the German Collection (based on a building from Saxony). I first became aware of this model some years ago and sketched up a simple plan from images on the internet. Recently, while browsing a charity bookshop, I picked up a hardback book called *The Cottages of*

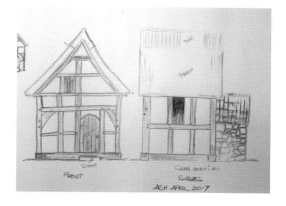

---

1   Lilliput Lane is a manufacturer of small decorative cottages or ornaments which are originally sculpted in wax and then cast in resin-hardened stone powder before being painted. They are sold as collectors' items and can command very high resale values.

Lilliput Lane and there, on page 165, was an official image of this quaint little model. I found my original doodle and using the new image in the book as well as images on eBay, I sketched up a more detailed plan.

If I was to sum-up my terrain model style or give an example of a typical 'Dampfpanzerwagon' scratch-build, it would be a timber-framed structure with a thatched roof and some stone detailing. The Small Bakery is a perfect example of this.

Construction

Construction started with some corrugated cardboard formers, glued together with my hot glue gun. I purposely made the core structure a little smaller than I had drawn in the main plan, as I find it easier to add layers of cardboard to the core and make it bigger than cut the core apart to make it smaller.

I added a smaller extension to the rear of the bakery; this was also constructed from corrugated cardboard and glued in place with the hot glue gun.

This cardboard core was then strengthened by adding strips of torn newspaper applied over PVA glue. I find that this method of construction is both fast and easily modified should I need to either add or cut away parts of the model. I always try to have a suitable miniature on my workbench when starting out on a new build as this helps me with door and window openings. I should also add that I try to build models or pieces of terrain that can be easily handled or stored—as a rough guide, most of my scratch built models can fit into a cube 6 inches x 6 inches x 6 inches.

I would normally have started by building the timber frame next, but in a departure from the norm, I choose instead to add the rough, stone-built extension. The stone walls were constructed from DAS modelling clay applied over dilute PVA glue and pressed in place in a haphazard manner. The DAS has been allowed to set in odd shapes and with no uniformity or regularity of thickness. I used a simple plastic sculpting tool to add some irregular gouges and odd stones to the walls.

It may come as a surprise to discover that I find sculpting odd or irregular stone walls much more difficult than regular or perfect layers of horizontal and rectangular stones. To get around this when modelling less structured stone walls, I place odd, irregular stones first and then, when the DAS is fully set, I carve more stones to join these up. As a general rule, if you think you are becoming too regular in your stone carving, stop and move on to another section or carve in the opposite direction or angle to what you would normally attempt. Triangular or five-sided stones force you to be less regular in the layers you sculpt.

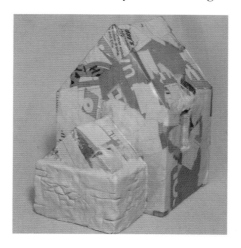

The stone wall was carved with a new scalpel and detailed with a large metal pin. I find that wetting the DAS can help with the carving. Prior to taking this image, I 'scrubbed' the DAS with a wire brush to give the surfaces of the stones a more natural look. The DAS stonework was then allowed to dry or harden off by placing the model on top of a radiator.

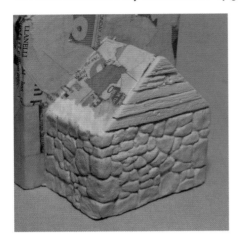

I used green foam to add the wooden sidings above the stonework on the back of the stone extension. The green foam was cut into layers and then thin strips before I added wood grain by scraping with a razor saw and brushing with a wire brush. The oversized green foam strips were glued in place with superglue, then trimmed back to the roof profile with a scalpel. Nail holes were added with the point of a needle pressed into the foam.

The timber framing on the main building was again built from textured strips of green foam. I recommend cutting the strips freehand (without the use of a ruler or straight edge), as the slightly irregular timbers add to the character of the building. The green foam timbers were glued in place with superglue and any gaps filled with DAS.

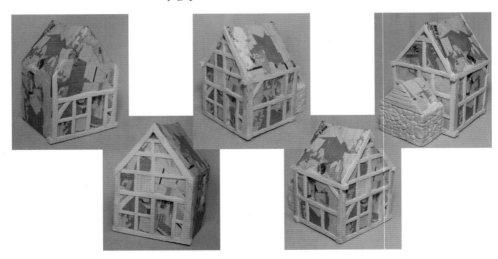

With the timbers in place, I filled in the wattle and daub areas on the main building with more DAS, which was applied over dilute PVA glue. To add some texture to these panels, I stippled the DAS with a stiff hog's hair brush before painting it with diluted PVA glue. I try not to model a smooth, flat surface on these panels, as I believe they look better with a little bit of surface texture and odd irregularities.

I also added tiny pieces of green foam to mimic the ends of tenon joints used in the construction of timber framed buildings; these tenon joint ends were further detailed with a scalpel and some sandpaper.

The main door was also sculpted from green foam.

With the core of the building constructed, I could have moved on to building up the thatch roof, but instead I modelled even more small details—this time, the wooden pegs which are also used in the construction of timber framed structures.

These pegs (I have also heard them called 'treens' or wooden nails) were constructed from cocktail sticks or tooth picks. I thin the cocktail sticks by trimming with a scalpel and then taper the ends before cutting them into sections about 5mm long. I have seen from real life examples that these pegs can vary greatly in both thickness and length.

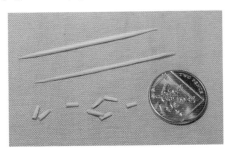

I drilled holes in the foam timbers with my Dremel set to high speed, and then inserted the pegs with a set of tweezers after dipping the ends in superglue.

I find that exaggerating the thickness of these pegs gives a more interesting surface texture to my models—if they were modelled to scale, they would be lost during the painting stages. For anyone wanting wooden pegs more in scale, you could try thin plastic rod or stretched sprue.

When I model my structures, I do not try to add every small detail or, in this case, every peg to every timber. Instead, I give an impression of the pegs by including most (but not all). I also like to leave the odd hole empty—call it a Dampfpanzerwagon trait!

The roof of the stone-built extension was next. I wanted to model pantiles or long, half-round clay tiles as the covering, but before adding these I built a sub-structure from thin strips of green foam. I have found that most pantile roof tiles are built up over a wooden sub-roof and I wanted to do the same. The textured green foam strips were glued in place with superglue.

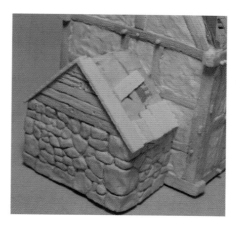

The pantiles are resin-cast sections that I had purchased via the internet and are the same as those fitted to the *pigeonnier* model featured earlier in this book. I have made scratch-built pantiles on some of my earlier models, but find the task too boring and repetitive; purchasing resin panels is so much easier. Even so, the resin pantiles are heavily modified. First, I hollow out the ends to better show the half-round profile—I use my Dremel drill set to high speed and fitted with a 1.5mm bit to 'carve' away unwanted resin. In addition I have 'distressed' the odd tile by damaging it with the tip of a scalpel and picking away at the resin.

Traditionally, pantile tiles got their distinctive shape from the fact that they were modelled on the thigh of the potter! The difference in colour is due to the variety of clays used, but also the temperature at which the tiles are fired.

The modified resin pantile roof sections had their base sanded flat and were then glued in place with superglue.

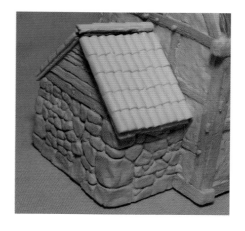

The top row or ridge is also a modified resin casting. I have taken one strip of pantiles and chamfered the bottom to fit between the two roof sections. Once again, this strip was glued in place with superglue.

The cement sections along the top of the roof and where the tiles join the walls of the bakery are detailed with thin strips or sausages of DAS modelling clay to mimic the cement fillets used on real buildings that feature these tiled roofs.

You can also see where I have added extra detailing to the wooden section of the upper stone extension. These details were modelled from more green foam and glued in place with superglue. Any gaps were filled with DAS.

The thatch roof was modelled from DAS modelling clay over corrugated cardboard formers.

I believe that DAS produces the best thatch roof effect on wargame models, much better in my opinion than the more common teddy bear fur that is currently in vogue. I added a sub-structure of corrugated card—this gives some 'body' to the thatch roof profile as well as saving on weight and DAS.

The first layers of DAS thatch were applied in thin, even layers over PVA glue, allowed to dry and then refined by carving and then adding more DAS. In the past, I have sped up the drying time by placing the sculpture in an electric fan oven at low heat for 10-15 minutes. However, in the last couple of months, we have purchased a new oven and I have been banned by Sue from using it for drying DAS!

I have produced an understated texture on the thatch roof, in keeping with the Lilliput Lane sculpt.

Referring back to the Lilliput Lane book and images on the internet of this particular model, I realised that the thatch did not go all the way up to the eaves of the roof; instead, there were a couple of layers of pantiles on the ridge. I had never come across this feature before—clay pipe tiles and thatch on the same roof—and thought it was worth trying to replicate on the model.

I have used the same pantile resin castings, cutting them down to just two layers and butt-joining them to fit the roof length. The pantiles were attached with superglue and when the glue was fully set, I built up the 'L'-shaped ends with more green foam to replicate a wooden sub-structure as seen on the bakery model. The ridge tiles were modelled in the same way as the stone extension roof and any gaps filled with DAS.

I noticed that the thatch on the Lilliput Lane model appeared to fit in under the pantiles. I modelled this by carving the thatch up to and under the pantiles, then brushing the join with a wire brush, adding more DAS and then starting again with the carving. I would be lying if I said that this was a simple five-minute job—in fact, it took many attempts and some considerable time before I was happy with the result.

Additional detailing was added to the roof eaves with more DAS modelling clay and strips of green foam. Note in particular how the top ridge has been tiled and blended into the pantile sections on either side.

The model was mounted on to an oval of 3mm thick plastic card. I like to add a spacer between the model and the base, in this case another piece of 3mm thick plastic card. I have used superglue and my hot glue gun for this join.

The groundwork was built up with DAS applied over dilute PVA glue and then stippled with a stiff brush.

I added a stone step to the front entrance. This was sculpted from a scrap piece of green foam detailed with DAS.

With most of the modelling complete, I now started on one of my favourite parts of scratch-building: the detailing.

The Detailing

The groundwork is sieved stones and sand applied over PVA glue, the small bench was modelled from green foam and the pot from my spares box. The sacks were sculpted from DAS and the bush or climbing vine to the rear of the building was sculpted from DAS. You should also be able to see where I have added plastic card detailing to the main door.

The openings on the first floor have been detailed with green foam doors glued in place with superglue.

Painting

I have not undercoated this model. The first colours applied were some red-browns over the exposed woodwork.

Then the stone extension was painted in muted grey before a darker wood stain was applied to the woodwork.

Next was the thatch basecoat. I used a mixture of Linen (a craft paint) and some Barbarian Leather to get an even mid-straw colour.

The thatch was highlighted with both Linen and a 'straw' coloured paint. In addition, I have toned down the red brown of the wood colour by drybrushing with a mix of mid browns.

The wattle and daub areas have been built up by painting with a slightly off-white acrylic paint. This was applied in a number of dilute layers to get an even coverage.

While the pantile roof tiles colour was built up with dilute red/orange/brown washes. The tiles were then drybrushed with a slight cream colour and the cement areas painted grey.

The groundwork was painted in my usual Snakebite Leather combination with odd stones and the front step picked out in grey.

The clutter items were painted next and to add some colour I have picked out one of the posts in orange clay. The sacks were painted in different tones to show off the sculpting and the bush was base-coated in dark green.

I thought that the white washed walls looked a little too stark, so I have 'washed' the lower edges with a pale brown wash. At the same time, the lower edges of the stone built extension were washed with the same colour.

The model was varnished with Galleria matt varnish

The base was decorated with dyed sawdust.

The Small Bakery is 95mm wide x 140mm deep and 1650mm tall. It is mounted on a 3mm thick plastic card base that is 180mm x 150mm.

Materials used

- Corrugated cardboard
- Card
- Green foam
- Resin Pantile roof sections (purchased from *The Lead Adventure* forum)
- Cocktail sticks (tooth picks)
- DAS modelling clay
- Plastic card
- Resin pots
- Sieved stones and sand

Paints used

- Red-brown craft paint
- Linen craft paint
- Straw craft paint
- Titanium white tube acrylic
- Barbarian Brown
- Beastly Brown
- Snakebite Leather
- Charred Brown
- Hot Orange
- Sun Yellow
- Dead White
- Black
- Stonewall Grey
- Forest Green
- Goblin Green
- Bone White
- Dead Flesh
- GW and Vallejo washes
- Galleria matt varnish

28/30mm
HUNGARIAN
CHAPEL

3.2
28/30MM HUNGARIAN CHAPEL

A Cardboard Church

Quite late on in the planning process for this book, I enquired if there was a model that the editor would like to add to my list of scratch-built projects. He suggested a church. As it turned out, I had already sketched up some plans for a mid- or eastern European church and, after searching out the original illustration, I re-drew more detailed plans.

I thought it would be interesting to set myself the target of building this structure from nothing but foam board and card to see if I could still get a good level of detail. With the exception of the single round bead and the two bamboo skewer finials on the roof, and using DAS and fine filler as a texturing medium, I have indeed succeeded in constructing the whole model from foam board and card. Very 'old school'.

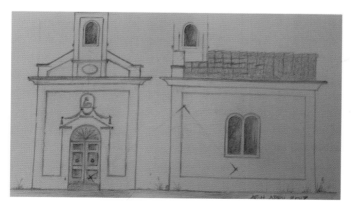

Inspiration

The church is based on an illustration found in the museum guide, *The Museum of the Hungarian Village at Szentendre*, photo 41— the Mosonszentjanos Votive Chapel (1843). As with many of my projects, I started with a planning sketch.

Construction

The main structure was built from black-faced foam board which I had 'squirrelled away' for just such an occasion. I transferred the simple rectangular profiles to the foam board and, with a new blade in my scalpel, I cut out each of the four sides. I used a T-square and a metal straight edge to ensure that all corners were true right angles, and a circular template was used to mark out the windows.

I thought that the foam board walls were looking a little too flimsy, and so cut a second set of foam board walls to act as internal strengtheners. This plain rectangle was glued together with a new hot glue gun, one that uses smaller glue sticks, but I found that my trusty and very well used old gun was far better as the glue had started to set before putting the pieces together. I find that the secret of using a hot glue gun is to make sure that it is hot enough to make the glue flow. Looking back, I can see no reason why PVA glue and pinning would not have worked just as well.

I also added an internal base of foam board to the four wall sections to ensure a square structure. One more tip when using a hot glue gun is to add extra fillets of glue to the inside corners of joints, which I feel strengthens the structure.

I trimmed back any glue that had dribbled through and started planning the decoration to the sides. For the main ledges to the top, bottom and sides, I used the backing card from a sketch pad. This was cut into long strips, again using a metal straight edge, and glued in place over-sized.

When the glue had set, I trimmed back the edges before moving onto the next side.

Remember to take into account the thickness of the card when measuring out the decorative overlays.

The uprights and upper decoration were also modelled from the 2mm thick card, while the detailing around the windows was cut from 1mm card. I used DAS modelling clay to fill any imperfections.

I used 1mm thick card to model the surrounds for the windows and the small decorative alcove above the door. These card layers were glued in place and then sealed afterwards with PVA glue.

I applied some DAS modelling clay, then fine filler, diluted with water and a tiny bit of PVA to both fill any gaps and apply a simple surface texture.

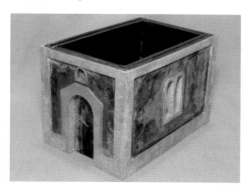

The sub roof was cut from 2mm card and again glued in place with PVA glue. The same card was used to add decoration to the front of the church.

At this stage, I decided to completely remodel the rear of the church. I had been searching the internet for inspiration as to what colour combination to use on this model, when I saw a similar church/chapel with an octagonal end. I knew at once when I saw the image that I needed to add this feature to my model.

I first cut off the rear of the church, then drew up some simple scale plans...

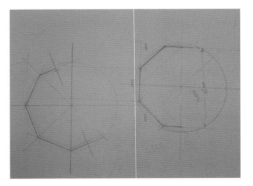

...and built the new angled church end from some more foam board. I decided to add a smaller single window to each of the three wall panels.

The new wall was glued in place with my hot glue gun.

I proceeded to add the 2mm card cladding to the top and bottom of the walls.

Then the upright corners, and finally the window surrounds and the new roof.

Texturing was done in the same way as the earlier updates. I think it is obvious how this new chapel end has turned this simple rectangle into a unique model.

A new upper roof was added from a layer of 5mm thick foam board, clad with strips card.

Then a second, decorative layer was added from 2mm thick card.

The tower was also built from 5mm thick foam board and 2mm thick card. I have used both my hot glue gun and PVA glue to stick the pieces together.

The decorative pillars and upper walls were constructed from foam board and card to match the lower wall. Once again, DAS and filler were used to fill any gaps and add texture.

The upper window surrounds were decorated with 1mm thick card, in the same way as the lower walls/windows.

The sub-roof for the sloping roof was constructed from corrugated cardboard and card.

I then used 1mm thick card for the cladding. I strengthened the sub-roof with strips of torn newspaper applied over PVA glue and sealed with more glue.

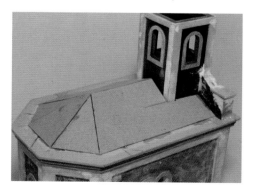 

Before starting on the roof tiles, I modelled the main doors and, in keeping with my plan of modelling the whole church from various thicknesses of card, I used card...

The door was glued in place and any gaps filled with DAS and filler. The tower roof was built from card in the same way as the main roof.

The main doorstep was built from two layers of card.

The Tiled Roof

In keeping with my aim of modelling the entire church from card, I choose to make this tiled roof from some 1.5mm thick card—an ex-advertising sign. I started by sanding the glossy surface with some fine sandpaper, then cut the card into ½-inch thick strips which, as you can see, were glued in place around the base of the roof.

I overlapped the tile strips, allowing just 10mm to show, and five layers later, the base of the tiled roof was finished. I didn't worry too much about a perfect join as my plan was to hide these joins with more card.

I then added small strips of 1mm thick card, each one running down the roof. I found that the best way to do this was cut a strip of card 8mm wide and use this to mark out the positioning of the smaller, vertical tiles. When this was done, I added each tile one at a time over PVA glue.

Far from being a chore, I found the exercise very relaxing.

I used some more card—this time the card from a toothpaste tube box—to add the overlapping strips at the edges of the tile joins. Once again, these were glued in place with PVA glue.

Any joins were filled with DAS modelling clay and I also added a round, wooden bead over a bamboo skewer to the top of the main tower, as well as a second bamboo skewer to the eaves of the larger roof.

The whole roof was given a covering of diluted PVA glue and fine filler, which was brushed on to the tiles in a 'stabbing' motion with a coarse hog's hair brush to add some additional texture. The fillets between the tiles and the uprights were modelled from DAS.

The Base

I used some spare 3mm plastic card for the base, as I did not want a card base to warp.

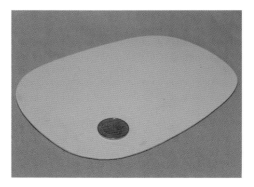

The base was roughly shaped with a scalpel before chamfering the edges by trimming with a knife and sanding smooth.

The cardboard church was glued to the base with my hot glue gun and the groundwork built up with DAS modelling clay over PVA glue. Additional texture was added by applying sieved stones and sand to the base and then adding some PVA glue which had been diluted with 'wet water' (water to which a drop of washing-up liquid had been added)—the washing-up liquid breaks the surface tension and allows the PVA glue to flow around the stones and the sand. When dry, this mix is very, very strong.

Still planning to make everything from plain card, I added three card headstones to the rear of the church, a feature I have seen on many churches.

Prior to painting, I used DAS, filler and PVA glue to fill any gaps or joins as well a seal the model.

Painting

The colours used were inspired by an image found on the internet.

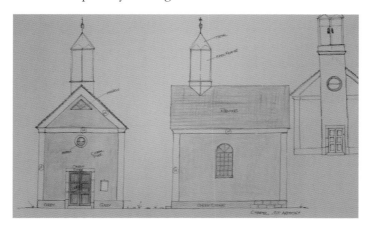

I used some artists' tube acrylic paint: Ochre mixed with Titanium White to lay down the undercoat/basecoat. I needed a couple of thin layers as the black foam board was difficult to cover up in a single coat.

Once I was happy with the finish, I started to paint the grey roof. Odd tiles were painted in a darker grey. Then the roof was drybrushed.

Now the white decoration. I used more Titanium White, but this time mixed with a tiny spot of black to block in the grey/white areas. A second layer was added, this time with more white added helped to define these areas.

Then a third layer, almost 100 per cent Titanium White, allowing some of the earlier layers to show through.

The white areas around the top of the walls were touched up with a smaller, detail brush.

I spent some more time drybrushing and detailing the roof, then painting the bamboo skewer and wooden ball.

The groundwork has been painted in the same Snakebite Leather/Snakebite and white mix shown in previous tutorials.

The door was painted brown and then drybrushed. I painted the three gravestones in combinations of grey.

The Stained Glass Windows

I have wanted to test out this technique for modelling stained glass windows for some time and the cardboard church gave me the perfect opportunity, using an old Christmas card. I cut in-fills for each of the windows and glued them in place with a small drop of superglue.

Then I decorated the base with dyed sawdust.

The cardboard church was great fun to both model and paint. By restricting myself to using just card, the project was not like any of the other models featured in this book—more like 'old school' card modelling that I so enjoyed back when I was building the cardboard structures featured in early *White Dwarf* articles. The model is 110mm wide x 160mm long x 40mm high (to the top of the spire). It is mounted on a 3mm thick plastic card base that is 150mm x 210mm.

Materials used
- Card (various thicknesses)
- Foam board
- Bamboo skewers
- Wooden bead

Paints used
- Artists' acrylic Ochre
- White
- Black
- Stonewall Grey
- Copper
- Bronze
- Snakebite Leather
- Galleria matt varnish

28/30mm
PENINSULAR
DIORAMA

3.3
28/30MM PENINSULAR DIORAMA

WORKING WITH FOAM—JUST FOAM

Inspiration

I have to admit that there is no one single point of inspiration for this particular model. An email from Pen & Sword suggesting I included a structure from the Spanish or Portuguese campaign had me searching through my scrap books for something I could model. I found many images and sketches which I have combined in this mismatch of different buildings to produce a self-contained diorama.

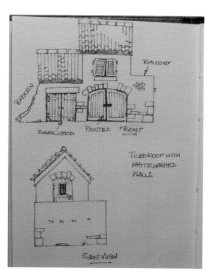

After seeing some scratch-built nativity scenes constructed from expanded or insulation foam, I set myself the challenge of producing the whole model from foam—scrap pieces of foam that I had in my stockpile. I could have used many different products to make these buildings, but forcing myself to use just one material has made me think about both the construction and the finish of this piece.

I keep a box filled with small off-cuts of foam in the corner of the shed for projects just like this.

The first attempt used 17 different pieces of blue foam to build the centre piece, but I was very aware that the model appeared too large and so it was back to the drawing board and a second building was constructed, this time about 10-15 per cent smaller than the original. Don't worry; I'm sure I will find a use for the earlier and larger block.

Both these buildings were constructed based on the same illustration using blue insulating foam—just one larger and one smaller version.

I have used a mixture of PVA adhesive and my hot glue gun, with joints reinforced with cut-down cocktail sticks and dressmakers' pins to build up the core. If you look closely, you can see that some of the cocktail sticks (either cut back or sanded smooth) appearing on the surface of the model.

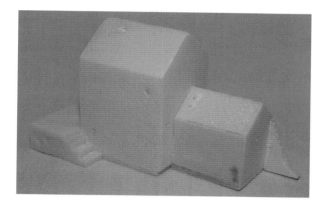

I now had something that looked more in keeping with the initial sketch, but I thought that the building looked a little too short and so I added a thin layer of foam to the bottom of the building which was also glued and pinned into place.

I used a scalpel (with a new blade) to add some initial surface features to this blank. A couple of doors and windows were cut into the blue foam, trimming small slivers from the foam and working across the whole assembly. This is a messy business but very satisfying.

I think it is obvious from the images that I have used lots of small off-cuts of foam, the stuff that is usually thrown away, to build this model. I'm sure it would have been easier to have constructed it from one large block or from corrugated cardboard as seen in earlier tutorials, but by now I was determined that this model would be made from foam, just foam...

In one of my sketch books (which are more like old fashioned scrap books) I had an illustration of a Spanish diorama, with some troubadours singing to a lady on a raised balcony and I wanted to include a similar, taller building with the first.

Once again I have used scrap blue foam to build the core. This was connected to the first with PVA glue and more cut-down cocktail sticks, pressed through the foam with the butt end of a pencil. As I looked at this rather large and unstable structure, I started to wonder how I would base it! I spied a silver-coated round cake stand that I had picked up in a charity store some time ago and the idea was born to build a self-contained diorama, rather than just a scratch-built model on a simple terrain base. The cake stand or base is 350mm across and 12mm thick.

Texturing

With the base structure now complete, the next stages were all about surface detailing. Firstly a word about detailing blue foam.

Blue foam is not the strongest of foam and in many ways not the best from which to construct detailed structures. It has a coarse, grainy texture that can show through on the finished model and does not like either superglue or hot glue, both of which tend to melt the foam. On the plus side, it is very easy to carve and takes impressed texture well.

I carve stone courses with a new scalpel by cutting a shallow 'V' into the foam and trimming the edges to round off the individual stones. Once this is done, I use a small wire brush to scrub the surface of the model and soften any abrupt joins or straight lines. Try to brush in different directions, as this gives a more natural look. I then use some fine sandpaper to remove the obvious burrs and impress a rough stone on odd surfaces. I might repeat each or some of these steps many times before I am happy with the result.

I have used DAS modelling clay and fine ready-mixed filler as additional surface texture and to hide the lumpy or coarse finish of the blue foam.

The blue foam building blanks have had corner stones added as detailed above, door and window openings have been carved into the surfaces and odd bits of spare foam have been glued in place to show misshapen rocks or stones.

I felt that adding this large structure to a 'normal' wargame base would have meant that it was unplayable, so I decided on a slightly different approach—the diorama base, as described above.

The flimsy buildings were both glued and pinned to the cake stand. I used Elmers and PVA glue, plus steel dressmakers' pins to secure the buildings to the base.

The base has had a couple of bits of cobbled stone textured wallpaper added. This is blown vinyl (foam) wallpaper picked up from a DIY store. I tore the pieces into odd shapes and glued them to the base with PVA glue then applied DAS modelling clay to blend the cobbles and groundwork together.

A layer of sieved stones and sand, applied in different layers over more PVA glue, completed the groundwork. My preferred technique is to paint on some dilute PVA glue and apply the stones and sand in layers. I then add 'wet water' (water to which a small drop of flow improver or ordinary washing-up liquid has been added) which has the effect of reducing the surface tension and allowing the water/glue mix to flow around the grit and sand to seal the texture in place. Remember that cheaper PVA glue is not waterproof and if you are going to use this technique, it is better to invest in a higher quality PVA adhesive such as Elmers or Unibond.

This was followed by more texturing. Now, a mix of PVA glue, fine filler and white acrylic paint was mixed up and painted onto the walls to smooth out the surface of the blue foam and give a more natural, plastered surface texture. I tend to start with a thick layer and continually add water to the mix, until in the end, I am using nearly 100 per cent water to smooth out the more obvious texturing.

Before moving on to super-detailing, I spent some time filling in odd areas with DAS modelling clay and applying a coarser groundwork texturing to some areas of the base by mixing up some sawdust and PVA glue. This mix was also painted on, particularly around the join between walls and groundwork.

The plastered walls were given a further surface finish by painting on a layer of Gesso. I find that this gives a better representation of roughly applied plaster and is a great undercoat for future paint finishes.

The octagonal/round well, which was copied from a design first seen in the TV series *Sharpe*, was constructed from a mix of blue foam and green foam pieces glued together with PVA adhesive and pinned in place with a couple of dressmakers' pins, before being painted over with a PVA, fine filler and acrylic paint mix.

Detailing

I have used the finer and less coarse green foam to add doors, window frames and sills to the buildings. I find that green foam can be superglued into position and, once set, I seal the pieces by washing with dilute PVA glue and some fine filler.

Nail holes were impressed with the point of a cut-down cocktail stick, while exposed nail heads were once again cut from slivers of green foam and glued in place with superglue.

I modelled the doors and windows from thin strips of green foam which was textured with the tip of a scalpel and by brushing with a wire brush. I had noticed while researching this model that vernacular Spanish, Peninsular-style buildings tend to be a bit less uniform than those in central Europe, with windows of different sizes, doors built from rough and even rotting wood, and roofs at all sorts of weird angles and built from differing materials. I have tried to replicate this on the diorama. This detailing continued until all the doors and windows had been finished. Once again, I have tried to use just foam.

The Roof/Roofs

The main sub-roof was built from more green foam. Thin, 2-3mm thick strips were textured with a wire brush and a scalpel. I was looking to reproduce the wooden roofs that are laid beneath canal tiles and, because most of this would be hidden under the main roof, I modelled this wooden sub-structure on the bottom and sides only. The central section was later filled in with some card, as I didn't want to waste my dwindling supply of green foam on an area that would not be seen (this is the only time I have used a material other than foam for the construction of this model).

The first full roof I modelled was the wooden planked roof on the tower extension, and I constructed this with strips of 2-3mm thick green foam which was, as usual, textured with a wire brush and a scalpel. I glued these individual pieces of foam in place with superglue and then detailed the top by adding two strips of foam wood which were modelled as upper supports to hold the planks in place.

Detailing was done by adding a DAS modelling clay fillet to the area between the upper wall and the wooden roof. I also filled any areas under the wooden roof with DAS and then textured these areas with a stiff brush. The nail heads are tiny squares of green foam and the nail holes were made with the point of a cocktail stick.

In earlier tutorials, I gave details of how I modelled canal tiles, using plastic beads, wooden dowel and plastic straws—even resin castings bought on the Internet. This time, I used green foam cut into 4-5mm thick strips, with the upper edge sanded into a curve and then scored and sanded to shape.

The exact technique is that I cut strips about 4-5mm thick. Try not to be too precise, as these tiles would have been made on site and would have varied. In fact, the first canal tiles were shaped by pressing against the thigh of the potter! These strips were sanded to shape and then detailed with the reverse edge of a scalpel to define the join between tiles. Prior to gluing in place, I used the tip of a scalpel to open out the lower edge and show the upside-down 'U' of the bottom canal tile. The tile strips were trimmed to shape and then glued in place with superglue.

When the main roof was finished I added a strip of canal tiles across the top or ridge before filling any gaps with DAS. Once the DAS was set, I washed the area with some diluted PVA glue as these small areas of green foam can be very delicate and the PVA glue wash gives it some protection.

The roof of the tower was modelled in the same way, but with longer strips of tiles.

With four of the six roof panels complete, I decided that the last two panels would be tiled with wooden strips—by which I mean foam strips, textured to *look like* wooden strips. I used more green foam and cut this into thin strips before texturing with the teeth of a razor saw and scratching or scrubbing with a wire brush. I then cut the tiles to size. The first tiles, or should I say 'planks', were glued in place and... Well, it was obvious to me that they were over-sized for the roof. I therefore removed these initial tiles/planks and started cladding the roof with smaller 5mm wide tiles.

I was much happier with the smaller tiles and continued to cover the whole roof with them. Once the main tiling was done, I added more green foam tiles to the eaves.

The canal-tiled roofs were then further textured by painting on a dilute mix of filler, PVA glue and acrylic paint, with a tiny touch of very fine sand (I use some Sahara sand that was brought back from Egypt by a very good friend) painted on with an old brush.

More Detailing

In my quest for even more detail—built out of foam—I have tried to add lots of clutter to the base. The wooden crates were modelled on some military cases I saw on the internet, seven pieces of green foam for each box or crate and then one opened crate with a separate top. The small wooden barrel was sculpted, or should I say carved, from green foam, with thin strapping also from green foam. The upturned boat was carved and sanded from even more green foam and the other bits were scratch-built in an evening's laid-back modelling.

Painting

I undercoated the whole model with some dilute acrylic white paint to which I had added a tiny drop of PVA glue.

In a change from the usual, I un-boxed my much underused Paasche H airbrush and base-coated the whole model with some watered-down Ochre acrylic paint. The finish wasn't fantastic, as the acrylic craft paint kept clogging up the airbrush nozzle. I finished off the painting with a large stiff brush.

The first highlights were roughly scrubbed on with a large and well-used brush—at this stage, I'm just trying to get the main colours laid down.

Next I added a layer of Linen—a craft paint that is a mix of Ivory and off-white. This was 'scrubbed' onto the walls with a large hog's hair (stiff) brush, which allowed the more yellow/Ochre colour to show through.

I added a second layer of Linen/white to further define the walls. Then started to highlight odd corner stones with various greys.

The grey stones were washed with a dirty black/brown wash to highlight the texture and reduce the 'toy-like' effect. In addition, you can see that I have started to paint the wooden roof on the tower extension.

The main woodwork areas have been painted in a green/brown mix and to add some variation, these areas have been purposely painted in slightly different colours.

The pantiles/canal tiles have been base-coated in various reds, brown, oranges and yellow. I have painted the main wooden tiled roof in a variety of different browns and greys to show worn or well-aged wood.

The canal tiles have been highlighted and odd stones picked out in grey. I like to allow the undercoated or base-coated colours to show through.

The windows were picked out in a dark blue/black colour, with Royal Blue highlights and a small highlight of white in the corner.

The groundwork was painted in a home-made mix resembling Snakebite Leather from Games Workshop (as my supplies were running low).

This groundwork was highlighted and drybrushed with a similar but lighter colour. Odd stones were picked out in grey, highlighted with white before being washed with a Sepia coloured wash.

The 'clutter' items decorating the base were painted in various browns and then drybrushed.

After varnishing with Galleria Matt Varnish, I decorated the base with static grass, static grass tufts and some ground foam, all glued down with superglue.

The Peninsular diorama was a real challenge to both construct and detail. Forcing me to use just foam was a great exercise in working with a simple, single material. It is based on a 350mm round cake stand. The smaller mariner's hut is 170mm wide x 90mm deep and 120mm tall. The tall tower is 100mm wide x 65mm deep and 160mm tall.

In terms of gaming potential, I would suggest that the whole diorama could be mounted into or onto a larger base—possibly a 2 foot x 2 foot terrain tile and the groundwork built up with DAS.

Materials used
- Foam
- Some card
- Sawdust
- Blown vinyl wallpaper
- DAS modelling clay
- Fine filler
- Cocktail sticks
- Dressmakers' pins
- Round cake stand

Paints used
- Titanium white
- Ochre
- Linen
- Stonewall Grey
- Black
- Grey White
- Ghost Grey
- Desert Yellow
- Leather Brown
- Charred Brown
- Orange Fire
- Sun Yellow
- Moon Yellow
- Beastly Brown
- Charcoal
- Magic Blue
- Goblin Green
- Dark Green
- Washes both bought and home-made

GLOSSARY

EXPLANATION OF TERMS AND MATERIALS

I am sure that there will be few terms or materials unfamiliar to any wargamer or miniature figure painter, but for completeness, here are some used throughout this book.

Abrasives
Sandpaper, 3M Sanding Sheets, Emery Boards, Wet and Dry Paper, Scotchbright etc. Used for sanding and adding texture to plastic card, foam or wood.

Accelerator
A liquid used to speed up the curing time of cyanoacrylate glue or superglues.

Acrylic Modelling Pastes
These artists' pastes are available in gloss, satin and matt finishes as well as a wide variety of different textured finishes. I suggest you browse the shelves of your local arts and craft store for inspiration. I use Daler-Rowney or Liquitex Medium.

Acrylic Paint
A water based paint that is waterproof when dry. Less harmful than enamels, with much faster drying times. The benefits are that the brushes can be washed out with water and they are easily available. I would always recommend that figures painted with acrylic paints should be varnished.

Blown Vinyl Wallpaper
Most DIY stores will sell (and sometimes give samples for free) a wide variety of blown vinyl wallpapers. Search through the different designs to see if there are any features that can be used for terrain making: for example, cobbled streets or flagstones.

Blue Foam
A generic term used throughout this book for firm foam (not polystyrene or white foam—packing foam), used as insulating material or for sound proofing, although there are some products intended for the professional model maker.

Clamps
I use G-clamps, D-clamps and spring-loaded clamps, but you can make do in most instances with simple wooden clothes pegs.

Contact Adhesive
Can be used for applying metal or plastic pieces to card or paper.

Core Structure
A term I use for the basic box onto which I sculpt or add detail. In most instances, my core structures will be corrugated cardboard glued together with a hot glue gun and reinforced with strips of PVA coated newspaper.

Cutting Mat
A 'self-healing' cutting mat is a common sense purchase. It acts as a protective layer to protect your work surface and/or your priceless antique dining table! I have a custom built workstation built to take an A2 cutting board/mat that I replace about once a year.

Cyanoacrylate
The general term used for superglue, also called 'Crazy Glue'! Bonds virtually any materials together (including skin) in seconds.

DAS Modelling Clay
A self-hardening or air-hardening modelling clay which comes in different sized packages and various colours. I usually try to add DAS to my models over a layer of PVA glue, as this improves adhesion and reduces the risk of shrinkage and cracking. Cheaper versions are available in craft stores.

Daylight or Craft Light
A light bulb that has a more balanced light, usually removing or filtering out some of the yellow light associated with traditional tungsten bulbs and adding blue light. This 'cooler' light gives a more balanced light spectrum which is ideal for both craft work and painting.
I have two 60 watt daylight bulbs in anglepoise lamps, one either side of my workbench.

Dental Tools or Metal Sculpting Tools
My favourite is the 'spear headed' sculpting tool which, along with a scalpel and a large needle, account for 99 per cent of my sculpting tool box. I find it helps to add a sponge handle to the metal shaft as this makes it easier to hold and causes less fatigue.

Dremel
The brand name of a miniature, hand-held electric drill; cheaper alternatives are available.

Drybrushing
A commonly used technique to enhance or highlight surface detail by gently 'flicking' the brush over the surface and applying paint to the high points only. For the very best results, it is recommended that you use a flat brush and the tiniest amount of paint.

Dyed Sawdust
Sometimes referred to as 'Railway Modelling Scatter'. I use a variety of Pea Green colours and makes to both cover my gaming table and decorate the bases of my terrain pieces.

Enamel Paint
Spirit based (rather than water based) paints. The most well-known manufacturer is Humbrol which is sold in small metal tins and requires White Spirit to clean the brushes.

Epoxy
A range of glues or fillers that come in two parts. For example, Araldite Glue or Milliput Epoxy Putty.

Flow Improver
An additive that helps 'break' the surface tension of water and can help with the flow of acrylic paints or PVA glue. As an alternative, you could add a tiny drop of washing up liquid to your brush cleaning water. I have been told that the cheaper the washing up liquid, the better the effect.

Foam Board

A paper/foam/paper sandwich used as lightweight backing card for presentations or in craft work. Foam board comes in a variety of different styles and qualities. The cheaper white foam foam board is great for basic construction, while the better quality (and more expensive) cream foam foam board has tougher foam that can be carved and textured.

Future or Klear

A clear, acrylic floor varnish which has dozens of practical uses for the model-maker, from producing home-made washes to acting as a base coat for transfers or decals and then as a seal over the top. I have used it as an additive for acrylic paints when you want a smooth, brush-strokes free finish.

Green Stuff

A two-part epoxy filler, one blue and the other yellow, which, when mixed together, produces a green putty. Used by figure sculptors and to sculpt fine detail. Small pieces of Green Stuff should be attached over a drop of superglue. There are many who suggest that a 60 per cent yellow plus 40 per cent blue proportion of Green Stuff is the best mix. I suggest that you experiment to find your own ideal mix. Curing time can be speeded up by placing the sculpt in a warm oven or under a lamp.

Ground Foam

Coloured ground foam can be made, but I buy mine from my local modelling store. When glued in place it can represent bushes, hedges or foliage. Try to vary the colours and grain size for a more natural effect.

Hot Glue Gun

A tool that melts sticks of thermoplastic glue and then dispenses it through a metal nozzle. As the glue cools, it hardens, making for a very firm and quick bond. Ideal for 'core structures' on which further detail can be built up. I prefer the more expensive hot glue guns, the ones that can be used as either mains powered or free-standing (without a flex). I also have a mini hot glue gun that I use for detailed craft work.

Kit-Bash or Kit-Bashed

A model that has been built with kit parts or using some modified kit parts, but not necessarily as intended by the manufacturer. See 'Scratch Built' for further details.

Laser-cut

A relatively new technique which uses lasers to burn through MDF or card to produce simple construction kits. In recent years, I have seen some impressive kits, produced for and targeted at the wargamer.

Milliput

Trade name of a two-part epoxy putty, perfect for modelling use, sculpting and filling. Comes in a wide variety of colours and finishes. I prefer Superfine White or Standard Milliput.

Oil Paint

Artists' paint medium. Used mainly by fine figure painters.

Olfa

A company that makes high quality cutting tools, for example a 'P' cutter—used for scoring and cutting plastic card; a circle cutter—used for cutting circles; and a beautifully balanced 18mm snap-off bladed knife—my favourite general purpose knife.

Pin Vice
A small hand held drill. I also have a model-makers' Archimedes twist drill which I found in an antiques shop.

Plastic Card/Styrene Sheet
Thin sheets of plastic which can be bought from model shops, but also scrounged from plastic packaging and advertising signs.

Plastic Rod
Strips of plastic which can have various profiles. As with plastic card, this can be shop bought but is also available at a fraction of the price if you search around. For example, cotton ear buds will give great plastic tubes. See also Stretched Sprue.

Polyfilla (Filler or Spackle)
A filler used for household repairs. It can be purchased as either a ready mixed tub/tube or as a powder to which you add water. I like to add a little PVA glue to my filler, while others add coloured pigment or paint. This helps if the terrain or surface is damaged, as the white filler will not show through.

Polystyrene Adhesive
Available in tube or liquid forms. Not one of my favourite glues, as the smell can be quite overpowering, but the liquid types have their uses when sealing scratch-built detail, for example plastic card rivets or door furniture. The glue actually 'melts' the plastic and as it dries, this forms a very strong bond. I keep a specially marked (old) brush for applying liquid polystyrene glue/solvent.

Primer
An undercoat, usually of neutral colour used as a fine base to apply subsequent layers of paint —used by figure painters.

PVA Glue
Poly Vinyl Acrylic. A type of glue, sometimes called wood glue or white glue, ideal for foam, cardboard and paper. Different versions are waterproof, cheaper versions sometimes have additives or thickeners. The better quality PVA glues are slightly more expensive.

Razor Saw
A fine-toothed model-making saw. The better ones cut on the 'pull stroke' rather than the 'push stroke'—the very best comes from a company called Zona. In most instances, a simple junior hacksaw will do.

Sanding Sticks
Strips of wood onto which I have attached abrasive paper (sandpaper) with double-sided tape. Some modellers use a wooden ruler. Ideal for both sanding and/or adding texture to plastic card or foam. I would also recommend that you build yourself a sanding plate, a sheet of wood or chipboard onto which you apply abrasive papers with double-sided tape. My own sanding plate is a piece of toughened glass—this allows you to sand individual pieces to a perfectly flat surface.

Scalpel
For example, Swann Morton handles and blades—ideal for intricate cutting and carving. I recommend the No.11 blade.

Scratch-Built

A term used by many modellers to describe a model that has been built without the use of a kit. In this book, the term means built from raw materials such as paper, card, wood etc and detailed with features that have been modelled by me, rather than bought or taken from another model or kit.

Set Square/Try Square

A measuring tool designed to create a perfect 90° right angle. I prefer a metal set square as I can use it as a guide when cutting or scoring plastic card.

Skin Detail or Surface Detail

A term that describes the sculpted detail on the surface of terrain models. It is my goal to cover every square inch of my scratch-built models with sculpted or modelled detail.

Snap-off Bladed Knife

Also called a box cutter, a knife that has a segmented blade which can be snapped off when blunt to give a new point. Ideal for most model-making work. Some modellers use a Stanley bladed knife.

Static Grass

Fine pieces of coloured nylon which can be glued in place to represent scale grass. Also available as static grass tufts. Try to vary the colours you use for a more natural look. Static grass can also be painted and/or drybrushed.

Stretched Sprue

Sprue is the spare plastic that is found on all plastic kits—we usually throw it away. This old technique is where sprue is heated over a candle and, when partially melted, stretched or pulled apart. With practice, you can get some very fine stretched sprue and it's free.

Undercoat

A layer of paint used as the base coat. In most of the examples in this book an undercoat will be Black or Dark Brown.

Varnish/Varnishes

I use two types of varnish: a gloss varnish as a protective coating (usually white spirit based, for example Ronseal Hardcoat) and a matt varnish (Galleria water-based matt varnish) as a matt coat.

Washes

Traditionally, diluted oil paint (black or dark brown) applied as a 'wash' to help define detail. Today there are ready-made oil based and water based or acrylic washes in many different colours and strengths, although a quick search on the internet will give you lots of home-made wash recipes.

Colour Washes
A technique where paints are watered down and applied in 'washes' over the figure or detail to accentuate surface detail or weathering.

Tint
Just that, a wash or 'filter' that just tints the underlying colour or paint, similar to looking through coloured lenses.

Filter
A very light or watered down wash (1 part wash to 20 parts plus of water or spirit) that is

applied to a single colour basecoat to subtly alter or modify the base colour by tinting it, while a Wash would 'pool' around sculpted detail and help define it.

Pin Wash

Another traditional wash applied in a focused area—for example, around the rivets or over the access hatches of a 1/35th scale tank, to detail the cockpit or wheels of a 1/72nd scale airplane, or for painting faces and hands on a 28mm wargame figure. A pin wash was used around the wooden pegs in the timber framed building to highlight this detail.

On the microscopic level, acrylic paint has a very rough texture and washes stick or pool to this texture; lighter highlight colours are therefore easily stained by these washes. Coating the surface with gloss varnish or Future and allowing it to fully dry before adding the wash can give better effects, as the wash stays in the valleys rather than on the ridges or in the shadows rather than on the highlights.

Washing Up Liquid

No, it's not a joke, but something that all terrain builders should have in their arsenal. Firstly, a tiny drop of washing up liquid in your water bottle will act as a flow improver for your acrylic paints. Secondly, Wet Water (see below, water with a drop of washing up liquid) can act as an additive to PVA glue when securing sand or gravel to a base. Apply your sand or gravel dry and then add a few drops of Wet Water either before or after you apply PVA glue, then allow to dry. Railway modellers have been using this technique for years.

Wet Brushing

Like Dry Brushing, but with lots more paint on the bristles—ideal for highlighting texture quickly and as a rough or first coat.

'Wet Water'

Water with a flow improver added—see Washing-Up Liquid above.

White Spirit

Mild spirit solvent, a substitute for turpentine, used to dilute enamel paints and/or clean brushes.